Defibrillator

www.stopheartattack.com
1-888-823-6967

Medtronic Technical Services
1-800-442-1142

Tony Franklin

The Tony Franklin
COMPANIES
Lexington, KY

The Tony Franklin Companies
508 East Main Street #407
Lexington, Kentucky 40508
www.thetonyfranklin.com
Email: tlf3c@aol.com
Fax: (859) 389-9340

Printed in the United States of America

Edited and proofread by Dana Brust

Final edit by Andrea McKeown, Writer's Lifeline, Inc.
www.thewriterslifeline.com

Cover and text design by Todd Detering
Crystal Communications
2009 Family Circle, Suite 3
Lexington, KY 40505
Phone: (859) 255-0076
www.crystalcommunications.biz

First printing: July 2005.

Library of Congress Catalog Card Number: 2005930612

ISBN: 0-9714280-1-8

This book is dedicated to Victor, Cheryl, Cortez, and Syreeta. I never knew you until tragedy brought our lives together. You have taught me lessons in love, forgiveness, and salvation. My life is truly blessed for having you in it, and to be chosen to tell your story.

Thank you for trusting me to share Victor's legacy with the world.

I love you,

Tony Franklin

Table of Contents

Acknowledgements

Writing this book was an act of love, not just from me, but from hundreds of people who gave their time and energy to make it possible to finish this project. Wayne Wood loved Victor Hill, just as he has loved hundreds of his students over his coaching and teaching career. Without his constant reminders to me, corrections to my grammar, and some simple persuasive urging to make subtle changes to the story at times, I'm not sure this project would ever have been completed. Cindy Pennington of Lexington, Kentucky provided me with advice that ranged from editing and style to finding a graphic artist. She was an honest and harsh critic, who is wise beyond her years and consistently pointed me in the right direction. Dana Brust, a single mother of a ten-year-old son, Jake, from Milwaukee, Wisconsin, was so moved by the story that her charge to me for editing and proofreading the book was totally dropped. She believes that one day her son's life will truly be blessed from reading this story and that the countless hours she spent correcting the poor English of an old coach (me), will pay dividends in her newfound lessons.

When this story was at a standstill because of my dire financial situation, and I had no possibility of spending the time needed to complete the project, I went in search of an angel: someone who would financially support the project until its completion. After numerous rejections, I went back to the "roots" of our country and pleaded with a home-town independent banker. I needed an angel who would base her decision to lend me the money to finish the project solely on her desire to help save the lives of young people and to tell the story of Victor Hill. Jo Etta Wickliffe, President and C.E.O of State Bank & Trust in Harrodsburg, Kentucky, became that angel and kept this story alive. Without her integrity and assistance, this book would never have been finished.

Chris Reid of Independence Bank in Owensboro, Kentucky, and Greg Bibb of Central Bank in Lexington, Kentucky believed in the possibility that this story could save the lives of young people in their communities, as well as throughout the United States. Both men assisted me in financially securing the printing cost. Without their heartfelt assistance, the deadlines would not have been met.

Lexington, Kentucky author Betty Ellison gave me sound literary and editing advice on several occasions. Bob and Gwen Grutza provided much needed assistance to me when the book was merely a dream.

The entire community of Hoover, Alabama, Victor Hill's family, and the hundreds of unnamed people who played a role in Victor's life will forever be remembered for making this story possible. Rush Propst made every contact I needed to make this book a reality.

Finally, without the incredible love and support of my family, none of this story would have been possible. My parents and my wife's parents continued to make sacrifices for us during hard times. My wife Laura continued to support a dreamer, instead of trying to mold me into something I can't be. My inspiration for everything good in my life continues to be my muses: my three daughters Chelsea, Caroline, and Caitlin. It is them who move me to never accept anything less than my dreams.

Introduction

Victor Dionte' Hill died from sudden cardiac arrest (SCA) on June 24, 2002, on the Hoover High School football practice field in Hoover, Alabama at the age of 15. I was on the field, conducting one of the many consulting sessions I do every summer in high schools throughout the United States and witnessed the dramatic rescue attempt, as well as his final gasps for air. There was no medical explanation for the cause of his SCA, and an entire community was brought to its knees as they searched for answers yet came up empty. His death was a tragedy I hope no parent, coach, player, or community ever has to endure again. His life, however, was simply remarkable.

After returning to my home in Lexington, Kentucky, I sat down one afternoon, approximately two weeks after the tragedy, and began writing. The writing was an attempt to help heal my troubled psyche, as I was having no success erasing the graphic images of Victor fighting for his life as his teammates and coaches helplessly looked on. After finishing sixteen pages, written on a yellow legal pad smeared with ink that had been watered with my tears, I attempted to read the words to my wife and daughters (ages 17, 14, and 12 at the time). Though struggling to overcome my emotions, I finally finished the final word and put the manuscript away, hoping this attempt at therapy would soothe my soul. I had no intentions of writing anything else, as I didn't know enough about his life to understand if it was a story worth telling.

It was over the next several months that I got to know Victor through the never ending stories about his life, which were relayed to me by his teammates, coaches, and friends at each new appearance I made during Hoover's remarkable march to the 2002, 6A State Football Championship. It was after more than a year of hearing these simple yet profound stories about his life and the everlasting positive effect he had on people's daily decisions that I decided to attempt to meet his family and see if they would be willing to allow me to spread his legacy to the rest of the world.

Victor's Victory was written because one young man's legacy of love, hope, dedication, and commitment to his fellow man was unique beyond words. In the short period of time he was on this earth, he made a consistent and dramatic difference in the lives of most everyone he met. When we select role models that we want to emulate, whether we are adults or teenagers, I suggest we look at Victor's life and begin there.

As you read this book, it is my hope that you laugh, cry, scream, and shout for joy-but mostly I hope you take immediate action to help save the life of another young person in your community. Victor's life was a purpose-driven life, and his death should also be made to have purpose. As you read this book, you will see that his death has saved at least one other young person's life already, and it is my hope that, through this book, he will save hundreds more.

Chapter 1

D-Day

I didn't speak to Victor as I passed him in the hallway. He was talking with teammate B.T. Hartloge, and they seemed to be occupied with each other's conversation. I knew I would have another opportunity to talk with both of them later in the day.

It was a beautiful Monday in late June of 2002, in the affluent suburb of Hoover, Alabama, a few miles south of Birmingham. The temperature was below 80 degrees, and the humidity barely noticeable, unusually comfortable for mid-June in Alabama. I had arrived on Sunday, one day prior, to begin my individual coaching sessions with Hoover High's future Parade All-American and University of Alabama quarterback John Parker Wilson, as well as his sophomore back-up Jarod Bryant, who would eventually earn the prestigious Mr. Football award in his senior season. This was my second year as a paid consultant to the Hoover football program, but I had been coming to Hoover since 1999 when Rush Propst became the head coach.

Victor Dionte' Hill (nicknamed "D" since early childhood) had been a standout running back in the Hoover football spring practices of 2002 and had caught my eye with his quickness and uncanny ability to make tacklers miss, similar to the style of former Detroit Lion's All-Pro running back Barry Sanders. I jokingly questioned Propst where he had been "hiding" this 15-year-old junior-to-be sensation. He assured me Victor was going to be the "real deal." There was no doubt in the coaches' or players' minds that Hoover High's quest for the 2002 Alabama 6A State Football Championship was going to be determined in large part by the role Victor would play. Little did any of us know just how big of a role he would play in their championship quest, as well as in the rest of our lives.

Victor was primed to become one of the state's top running backs, and he welcomed the role of becoming "the man." He laid in his bed night after night visualizing taking the hand-off and going eighty yards for the winning touchdown in the state championship game. He wanted the ball in his hands!

After an unexpected ankle injury to starting defensive back Gevar Bonham, those dreams came to an unexpected halt when Propst decided to move his best available athlete, Victor, to defense. While lying in bed and dreaming of Hoover High's championship games, Victor hadn't been dreaming of intercepting a pass and returning it for the winning touchdown. No, he wanted the ball! He was the running back in all his dreams.

A selfish player would have said no to Propst's request to move to defense, or at the very least pouted. He would have begged to fulfill his individual dreams and goals. But Victor dreamed of Hoover championships, and he loved and respected Propst.

When he lined up as the left cornerback with the first team defense on the first play on that Monday afternoon, it would be with a sly grin on his face, not a disappointed or selfish frown, because he was a starting varsity player on the Hoover Buccaneers. One of his childhood dreams had come true, and now he was ready to make his biggest dream come true: back-to-back state championships. He was ready to play!

I walked onto the practice field at 1:45 P.M. and remembered thinking what a mild day it was for late June in Alabama. Victor was going through some light warm-ups with defensive coordinator Todd Watson.

At 2:02, he jogged over to get a drink of water before the 7-on-7 passing drills were to begin at 2:06. I still hadn't taken the time to say anything to Victor, as I was focusing on my work with the quarterbacks. I was one of the many people drawn to his personality and charisma, and was seeking a selfish "refreshment" from an anticipated conversation with him. He was the type of player that kept coaches eager to work with young people.

Victor lined up in zone coverage for six of the seven snaps and man coverage in the single remaining snap. Barely a sweat was broken by any of the players in this informal summer ritual, which is performed at high schools throughout the country during the summer days in preparation for their upcoming fall football schedules.

"D's" DOWN

"Get up, D," I heard some of the players demand. I turned to see Victor resting on both knees in the defensive huddle.

"Come on, D, quit playing," bulky 245-pound linebacker and future University of Alabama defensive lineman Curtis Dawson shouted.

Defensive assistant coach Chet Knippers requested that the players back away and give Victor more room. I walked over and stood directly over him, thinking how unusual it was to see a player in such tremendous physical condition struggle so early in a workout, especially on a mild day.

Coach Knippers was joined by Coach Watson, and they commanded Victor to relax and slow his breathing down, as they began to help him lie down, while he rolled over on his back.

Several times in my twenty years of coaching I had witnessed a player struggling with the heat or the running, so I wasn't completely alarmed by the possibility of Victor having problems. Early in my coaching career I had experienced a day when two players went down at the same time with heat exhaustion and were taken away by ambulance.

Today, though, was eerily different. Victor was in top physical condition, and the heat and strenuous activity were nonexistent. The team hadn't done enough running to make a 300-pound offensive lineman breathe hard, so there was no way a 163-pound perfectly conditioned athlete should be struggling. The players didn't have on their usual twenty pounds of equipment that make a football player's body temperature much hotter than normal humans can imagine.

No, this was a relaxed, easygoing session in shorts and T-shirts that couldn't have caused any heat-related stress this quick. Maybe it was something he ate?

Knippers, myself, and Watson continued to talk to Victor in a futile attempt to get a vocal response. Although unsuccessful, no panic set in. All the coaches were concerned yet firm in their confidence that he was going to be okay. I pressed my left thumb and index finger on his throat, attempting to locate a heartbeat from his carotid artery. A light but consistent beat was visible and steady as I breathed a sigh of relief.

Victor's going to be okay, I repeatedly told myself. I even silently wondered to myself if he was faking it. I had seen players over the years do many things to get out of a practice session, and I hoped he was one of them.

Watson and Knippers continued to talk to him, while tapping his hands and moving his arms in hopes of getting a response. They got nothing in return.

Assistant coaches Craig Moss and Matt Moore had moved the remaining players approximately twenty yards down field, following a pre-rehearsed emergency plan from their CPR training classes. Moss immediately called 911 and requested an ambulance, while Moore called athletic trainer Brandon Sheppard, all within one minute of Victor taking his first knee.

Seconds seemed like minutes, and minutes seemed like hours as we continued to work, hoping for a response.

Watson tested for a pulse and requested I do the same. We both were unable to get a response and decided to begin CPR, with Watson doing the rescue breathing and I responsible for the chest compressions.

Okay, Tony, this is real. Just stay calm. Twenty-five years of CPR training. Find the xiphoid process, just below the sternum, make a fist and start compressions slightly above it at a 5-1 ratio, I silently recited to myself. My heart wasn't beating fast, and I was calmer than I could ever imagine. Why, I still don't know to this day.

Jesus! Can this be real? It doesn't seem real, I thought.

Watson cleared the airway and, as he approached Victor, Victor seemed to make an attempt to gasp for air.

Thank God! He's alive and aware! He just doesn't want Watson to put his mouth on his, I thought.

"Breathe, D, breathe! You can do it," all the coaches encouraged at the same time.

Total stillness. No response, no pulse, no movement.

Dammit! Come on, God. This isn't supposed to happen. Not to good people. Not to young people with character and innocence in them. My mind was grasping for a reason as I thought with a certain disgust at the possibility of a God that would allow this young man to die.

Once again, Watson lowered his mouth to Victor's. Once again, he gasped and breathed a deep cleansing breath.

"Breathe, D, breathe!" all of us commanded, still with little or no visible desperation in our voices.

No movement. No sigh. No air. No pulse.

For the third time, Watson lowered his mouth to Victor. For the third time he gasped and inhaled his deepest breath yet.

"Breathe, D, breathe!" We were singing in chorus now, a louder and more demanding voice, as if our volume might be heard by God if we just asked loud enough.

Out of the corner of my eye I caught a glimpse of an "angel" running toward us. It was Sheppard, who, like most of the Hoover staff and high school coaches and trainers throughout the country, is unpaid for work in the summer and was on campus just in case any of the school athletic programs needed him. I breathed a sigh of relief. Everything was going to be okay now. We had a professional medical person in control. Sheppard was the best trainer I had worked with in my twenty years of coaching. He would make everything work!

Ten to twenty minutes seemed to have passed since Victor went down (I would later learn that less than two minutes had elapsed from the time he collapsed until Sheppard arrived). Why is it that misery always seems agonizingly longer than reality, whereas joy often escapes without us recognizing its existence?

As Watson took over my position, the relief I felt was two-fold over Sheppard's arrival: I truly believed Sheppard held the same status as a doctor. High school trainers have responsibilities that sometimes resemble an ER unit, and Sheppard was the best. I was also thankful, in a selfish way, that my not yet attempted duties at chest compressions were now being taken over by Watson.

Would I have choked? Would I have failed to carry out my duties properly? Would Victor die because of my inadequacies? My subconscious asked me those questions numerous times after Victor went down. I was relieved I wouldn't have to worry about that scenario.

"D! D!" Sheppard repeated as he reached for his carotid artery in search of a pulse.

"Let's start," Sheppard told Watson as he cleared Victor's airway and approached his mouth.

Again, my brain told me he was simply tired or sick to his stomach. Each approach to his mouth brought the same gasp for breath. He simply didn't want their mouths to touch his. I couldn't have been more wrong.

"GASP, GASP," Victor once again responded to a mouth approaching his, as if to say he could breathe own his own.

"Breathe, D, breathe!" Sheppard commanded.

No response. No more breathing. No more gasp. Eyes shut. No pulse.

"Let's go!" Sheppard told Watson as he again moved his mouth toward Victor's.

This fifth approach to his mouth brought no gasp. No deep cleansing breath. Was that last gasp for air going to be his final one?

Pump—1, 2, 3, 4, 5—blow—Pump—1, 2, 3, 4, 5—blow.

Sheppard and Watson looked like a machine. It was like watching a CPR training class, only this time it wasn't a dummy. It was way too real. They performed with perfection. They were cool, methodical, stoic and professional.

God, this can't be real. It seems surreal. I hope it's a dream, I thought.

I've had those kind of dreams before, the kind that when I woke up, I believed they were real, only to find out later I had been sleeping.

"Please be one of those dreams. God, are you listening? Don't you hear those young men, some barely in puberty, praying their hearts out? This would be a perfect time for one of those miracles that you perform on occasion. Just think of what these young men would do for you, God, in the future, if you just let their friend breathe. Just let him live," I mumbled to myself, with desperate visions now swirling in my head as I watched Watson and Sheppard continue their methodical attempt to bring Victor back.

Where's the damn ambulance? It has to have been at least an hour now, I wondered to myself. I would later discover that the hour in my head had only been seven minutes in real time.

Eighteen young men joined hands and took a knee. They joined one another in the deepest moment of prayer they had ever engaged in during their young lives. Reality had smacked them in the face firmer than any religious ceremony or teacher's lecture could ever have prepared them for.

As I glanced at Victor's innocent Hoover teammates, I became acutely aware that they, like me, realized for the first time since he went down that he might die while we watched in helpless despair.

Glancing to my left, I witnessed a selfless and humane act by a television reporter. He stopped filming the rescue effort once the CPR attempt began on Victor, and was now in silent prayer with genuine and caring tears rolling down his face. A lesser man might have seen this as a career opportunity and continued shooting Watson and Sheppard's performance in an attempt to sensationalize what could become a lead-in dramatic story for the nightly news.

I heard the sound of an ambulance and searched for its arrival. A few minutes later, I saw the emergency medical squad driving onto the field under the direction of Coach Moore. They unloaded the medical equipment at a furious yet professional pace and placed it beside Victor as Watson and Sheppard continued CPR.

Thank God! Finally! Look at the equipment. It's just like a scene from the television show, *ER*. Victor is going to be okay now. This has to work, I hoped.

The EMT staff told Sheppard to stop the rescue breathing as they stuck a medical device (intubator tube) deep down Victor's throat. Sheppard replaced Watson and continued chest compressions as the EMTs placed an oxygen mask over Victor's mouth.

All these experts, all this medical equipment, and all these prayers – he has to wake up now. He has to be okay. He has to breathe again! He has to live! I told myself.

The EMT team was moving with precision and speed, but still his heart wouldn't beat.

"Stand back," an EMT told Sheppard as he hooked up the tiny electrodes of the defibrillator across Victor's chest.

"Clear," he said, as the 200 volts of electricity lifted Victor's body slightly off the ground.

No response. Lifeless. Nothing. My God, he is going to die,

I thought, believing it for the first time since he had taken a knee.

"Clear," the EMT said, as 300 volts shocked throughout Victor's body.

No response!

"Clear! Clear!" he demanded twice more, as he attempted to revive Victor with 360 volts and more.

Nothing. No response.

Sheppard stood up, never stopping the chest compressions as the EMTs loaded Victor onto the gurney and into the ambulance.

I can still see Sheppard's methodical pumping of Victor's chest as they closed the door and drove off the field. At the same moment, a dark blue pickup truck driven by Propst arrived.

Players looked like zombies. Coaches looked like ghosts. They continued attempts to be strong and everyone tried to keep the faith that Victor was alive, but their faces told a different story.

THE HOSPITAL

Propst had been attending a corporate event when his Nextel two-way radio-phone beeped with an incoming call from Moore telling him Victor had gone down and that he needed to get to the practice field immediately. As he drove onto the Hoover practice site, there was no way he could have prepared for the scene he entered: players in trances, an ambulance exiting his practice site with one of his favorite players having his chest continually compressed by his good friend and loyal trainer, and his assistant coaches hanging their heads in despair.

This graphic and vivid picture would remain in Propst's brain longer than he would care to recall.

I met Propst in the spring of 1998, while recruiting in Bayou La Batre, Alabama (yes, the same town of "Bubba" from the movie *Forrest Gump*) for the University of Kentucky, where

I had been an assistant football coach for one season. We had immediately hit it off and become friends, remaining as such through my four-year Kentucky coaching career. Afterwards, we mutually helped each other, as I spent numerous days helping him and his coaching staff learn and perfect my offense. And as his success and championships mounted, he helped me build my consulting business.

I told Propst to give me his keys and I would drive him to the hospital. Ninety, 95, 100, 105 miles per hour - I had not driven over 100 mph since my race to a hospital to see the birth of my youngest daughter, Caitlin, twelve years earlier. Driving 105 mph didn't seem that fast as I weaved in and out of the heavy I- 459 and I-65 traffic. I was as fearless as, and more foolish than, a NASCAR driver. My brain believed if we got there fast enough, Victor wouldn't die. If God knew we were risking our lives driving at breakneck speeds to get to the hospital, maybe He would open Victor's airway and give him life.

Propst jumped out of his truck and ran into the emergency room while I parked. When I entered the ER, I was directed into the waiting room, where I heard the desperate wail of a woman. The noise I heard prompted a flashback to December 1975, when two of my best friends, Ernie Rickard and Curt Jones, were tragically killed in an auto accident and another close friend, Ricky Williamson, was critically injured. I heard Ernie's mother and sister helplessly wailing the same cry, a grueling sound that pierced my eardrums and ripped into my heart.

Victor's mother Cheryl had been called as soon as he'd gone down on the field. When she arrived at the hospital, she had an empty and helpless feeling, still unsure exactly what was wrong and how serious it was. Cruelty was exhibited by a hospital policy that prevented her from seeing, embracing, or gently caressing her son while the medical team attempted to revive him.

Family, Victor's teammates, and parents began to flood the waiting room. Silent prayer, group prayer, and team prayers filled the hospital lobby.

After several minutes passed with no answers that satisfied her, Cheryl made a frantic and desperate dash for the doors that separated her dying son from her. When confronted by an older man (probably in his 60s) who once again denied her access to her son, she launched an overhand right, which if it had landed, might easily have placed another person in the ER. She had desperately tried to force her way in to see the beloved son she had sent to school that morning full of health and vigor. Gently yet firmly she was intercepted and restrained by Propst.

The emotional turmoil finally took its toil, and she collapsed and slowly crumbled the ground, with her knees as stable as rubber. She landed in the arms of Hoover High All-American and future University of Florida Gator wide receiver Chad Jackson, who made his most tender and valuable catch of his storied career.

Jackson held the grieving mother of his close friend and teammate (so close that they had begun to refer to each other as cousins only weeks before) safely in his arms, as he guided her into a private family room. He comforted her and held her securely, and more tenderly, than any of his many touchdown receptions in his decorated young life.

Time ticked by slowly with no word. Team physician Dr. Bill Bryant, father of Jarod, had been performing surgery when he was relayed the news of Victor's medical problems. His mere presence was somewhat soothing to many of us, much like when I was a child forty years earlier and my local hometown doctors,

Ralph Cash or Ed Settle, would arrive just in the time of need.

Dr. Bryant didn't have any good news, but many of us felt better anyway. There is a pure trust when you personally know your doctor. He is more than just a regular physician. He cares for you and your family and is comforting in ways we never understand until we move away and lose this simple, unappreciated benefit.

I walked outside the hospital doors to breathe some fresh air. Within moments, all hell broke loose. Victor was pronounced dead. That wailing noise now reached a level of intensity that would break the coldest of hearts, and it pierced my heart deeper than I wanted to admit.

Men aren't supposed to show their tender emotions; coaches aren't supposed to have them. These coaches, most under the age of 40, were ripped apart. Yet as they saw the players, families, and parents struggle for reasoning that didn't exist, they knew their time for mourning would have to wait. They would have to remain strong. If they showed weakness now, all of their past and future speeches about strength and character during adversity might be seen as mere words.

A female member of Victor's family waved her arms and mumbled to Jesus as she proceeded to walk directly into an oncoming traffic surge in the Birmingham rush hour. Watson, although still numb from his failed rescue attempt, had remained in control of his emotions and was closely following her in case she lost it. His instincts proved prophetic, as he made a lifesaving grab by he snatching her arm and pulling her away from the traffic, narrowly missing an oncoming car.

Young men from the ages of 12 to 18 witnessed two hours of reality that would change their lives forever. Their sense of invincibility had been shattered in a method no one should have to witness, especially those in their adolescent prime. Football, dating, and casual time would never be the same for those young teenagers who witnessed the dramatic rescue attempt and tragic death of one of their own.

THE CHURCH

God, what do we do now? Moments before Victor's death was announced, some players and parents had moved to Hunter Street Baptist Church in Hoover. I suggested to Propst we go back to the school for a few moments and collect our thoughts.

I pulled out a white pad and began to document the events as they unfolded. The accounting of every moment needed to be recorded while they were fresh on our minds. We needed to make sure, for Victor's family and for our present and future peace of mind, we had done everything possible—and correctly—to save his life.

We drove to the school without saying much to each other and spent thrity minutes reconstructing the events and putting the timetable together before leaving for the church.

The church was full of family, both the Hoover family and Victor's. Everyone attempted to soothe one another's hearts as they searched for answers. Religious professionals and counselors worked with anyone willing to accept their help, searching for ways to explain the unexplainable.

Dr. Bryant, Sheppard, I, and six of the Hoover coaches went to a back room to recount the events. I was stunned by the results of the timetable. After checking the phone, 911, and emergency team records, what I was sure had been forty-five minutes to an hour had merely been eight minutes.

2:06 *D went down*

2:07 *911 called by Craig Moss, Brandon Sheppard called by Matt Moore, Cheryl Hill called by Matt Moore, Coach Propst called by Matt Moore*

2:08 *Brandon Sheppard arrived and CPR began*

2:14 *EMTs arrived*

After we put the clock together, I spoke.

"Dr. Bryant, did we wait too long?" I began to sob uncontrollably while asking the question. "He was breathing, but should we have started CPR earlier?" I stuttered the words while attempting to regain my composure.

"Tony, you guys did everything by the book. It probably wouldn't have made a difference if this happened at a hospital. You'll always second-guess yourself and wonder 'what if.' That's natural. Don't! You coaches did everything right. Some things are simply unexplainable, and we may never know why Victor died," Dr. Bryant replied.

I didn't know if Dr. Bryant was being totally truthful, and I don't think any of us knew at the time if we did everything exactly the way it should have been done to save Victor's life, but I do know this: Dr. Bryant provided all of us with some immediate comfort that we desperately needed.

After regaining my composure, I felt that same safe and warm feeling of youth when Doctors Settle and Cash told me everything was going to be all right.

God, I wish for those days again, days when our doctors actually knew us and would take the time to genuinely and personally care for us.

All the coaches looked at one another. I knew a bond had

been formed that would place us in a small fraternity that none of us wanted to belong to: the fraternity of coaches who had watched one of their own die while feeling completely helpless. God, I wish I didn't belong to that fraternity.

We re-entered the main church and scattered. All the coaches had a wife, loved one, or special friend to comfort them. Although I was a friend of the coaches, and many of the players had known me for a couple of seasons, I was still a visitor. This was not my home, but in my three years of consulting and visiting, it seemed like an extended family to me.

I sat in the back of the church in a pew by myself. God must have known I needed help. He sent me Jessica, a young girl probably around 16 or 17 (close to the age of my oldest daughter Chelsea) and a school friend of D's.

"Were you there today?" she asked.

"Yes," I replied.

"D called me a few days ago. I didn't call him back," Jessica whispered, as tears began to flow down her young cheeks.

"He knows you loved him, Jessica. He knows you care. He feels your love for him right now. Don't feel guilty. We always wish we had done something else," I said.

The words flowed from my soul as I tried to comfort her. I wanted to soothe her heart. My mind continued to rewind to December, 1975. I have always wondered why I didn't call Ernie that morning. Maybe he wouldn't have gone on that deadly joy ride if I'd given him another choice. No matter how many times I play the scenario over in my head, he is still dead.

"Jessica, Victor didn't suffer. He was not in pain. His life was special. Don't regret what you didn't do with him. Be thankful for the times you shared," I implored, with the experienced voice of a remorseful man who had second-guessed himself for twenty-seven years.

"Thank you. I appreciate you talking to me. I feel better now," she sighed and walked off to join her friends.

I looked around the church and saw the unique love and influence one young man had accomplished in fifteen short years.

Breathe, Victor! Breathe, Victor! Should we start CPR now? Did we wait too long? I continued to play the scenarios over and over in my head as I searched for a reasonable explanation to the day's events.

I placed my head between my legs and began to weep. A hand touched my shoulder, and I looked up. Blake Davidson, star quarterback for the Hoover Buccaneers during the 2001 season, and Samford University quarterback today, provided me with a touch that instantly comforted me. We had built a special relationship in the summer of 2001, when Blake needed some extra work to earn the starting quarterback position for the 2001 season. After spending five days together, our relationship became more than just player/coach, as I considered him to be a friend, and he the same. We had continued to stay in touch after Davidson earned his scholarship to Samford University, located in Birmingham.

"Are you okay?" Blake asked.

"I'm good, Blake. It's great to see you. It was such a tragedy," I answered.

I attempted to regain my composure, feeling guilty for showing my emotions so openly around young men whom I felt needed me to remain composed and strong. We small-talked for a while, and Blake eventually left with his family. His presence and caring hand had provided me with a much needed touch at the perfect time.

GOING HOME

Two days later I began the six-hour drive back to my home in Lexington, Kentucky. As I drove, I wondered if the Hoover football family would be able to overcome this tragedy and move on with their attempt to win the 6A State Championship. No one could blame the coaches or the players, if their hearts were cluttered with confusion—or even bitterness. If their minds were filled with fear, even the harshest football critic would be empathetic. How does one overcome the unexplainable and mysterious death of a 15-year-old "special" teammate, especially when many of them had watched him take his last breath on the very practice field they would have to return to in two weeks to begin practice?

What would Cheryl Hill's life be like? Can any of us explain the feeling of despair and hopelessness that she would be burdened with for the rest of her life? Would she seek justice by filing lawsuits against the coaches, Hoover High, or the medical team, all of whom had failed to save her son's life?

The answers to these questions would come over the next three years, as each group battled with their own personal struggles while continuing their daily existence without this special young man whom everyone had come to know as D.

Chapter 2

Momma's Nightmare

Victor Dionte' Hill was prematurely born August 18, 1986, weighing only two pounds. He was so small, he fit into a nurse's hand.

It wasn't long before the nurses nicknamed him "wild man" because of his continuous wiggling, kicking, and rolling. He may have been premature, but he was anxious to make his presence in the world known.

By the age of three, Victor's vocabulary was full of colorful words, but the one he constantly spouted from his vocal cords was "football." He would stand looking out the windows at home and watch the older kids playing outside, and continue to repeat the word "football" over and over again, until Cheryl or Victor's dad Andre (who spent hours teaching his son the fundamentals of the game) eventually gave in and sent little Victor out to play with the "big boys."

By the time Victor finished playing little league football in the fifth grade, he had been given the nickname "Sugar Hill," and was a star running-back for the Tarrant Wildcats. He still had the trademark wiggle his nurses had recognized early on, while caring for him in his incubator, but had turned the wiggle into a running style that made him one of the most elusive running backs in the Birmingham area. Some of the area coaches, experienced experts in this football-rich state, began to sing the praises of Sugar Hill and mentioned his name as another potential star player for the Birmingham area.

By the time he reached middle school, the only question was whether he would remain a running back or become a defensive back. No doubt, defensive and offensive coaches would one day fight over which side of the ball was going to utilize his versatile and considerable skills.

After a four-touchdown performance for Hoover High as a sophomore against bitter rival Spain Park, the question of which side of the ball Victor would play seemed to be answered forever. The 2001 Hoover Buccaneers would go 14-1 and finish the season as the 6A state runner-up. That one loss, however, would keep him motivated to the point of obsession. His off-season was spent working out with weights and conditioning, while plotting the formula to secure 6A state championships for his junior and senior seasons. Most people didn't believe the goals he had written entering his ninth grade season, which boldly stated: "Win the state championship every year I am in high school, especially my senior season, and make sure my little brother Cortez stays out of trouble and is a good person." Victor included Cortez in everything he did, and his personal goal sheet was no different.

When the spring football practice of 2002 was finished, Victor was happier than he had ever been in his fifteen years of life. Not only was he going to be a starter on the Hoover High varsity, he was going to be the man with the football in his hands. He truly believed that fairy tales do come true, and his trademark smile shone brighter than ever before.

THE DREAM IS ADJUSTED

Senior defensive back Gevar Bonham fell to the turf awkwardly during a summer drill, and when the trainers and doctors announced he had severely fractured his ankle, the Hoover coaching staff knew they had a dilemma.

Every great Alabama high school coach knows that defense wins championships and if you have a weakness at defensive back, even the most inept of opposing coaches will find that defensive back and exploit him for a cheap touchdown and a victory. Propst and defensive coordinator Watson both agreed the move had to be made. Victor would have to give up his dreams of being the star running back and sacrifice for the sake of the team. It was now up to Propst to break the news to Victor.

"D, you know about the injury to Gevar," Propst said, as Victor looked directly into his eyes.

"Yes, sir," he responded.

"You are the best we got D, and although I know how much you love to play running back, the team needs you to play defense. How you feel about it?" Propst asked.

"Coach, I'll do whatever's best for the team," D answered.

He wasn't enthusiastic, but his answer was firm, and his eyes never left Propst's.

"I knew you would feel that way. Thanks, now let's get to work!" Propst exclaimed, as he shook Victor's hand when he stood up to leave the office.

Victor went home that night and confided in his best friend: his mother. "Mom, it's not fair. All my dreams, and my work to be the best running back, and I'm not going to even get a chance. Mom, I've even been practicing my moves on Play Station. I know it's the best thing for the team, Mom, but what about me?" he asked.

"D, talk to Coach Propst and tell him how you feel. He'll understand. Maybe there's somebody else who can play defensive back," Cheryl encouraged her son.

"Mom, I am the best one for the job. It doesn't seem fair, but I've got to do what's best for the team," Victor answered. "And you know something else?" he probed with a sheepish grin growing across his face.

"What, D?"

"I'll be back at running back, too. I'm just too good! They'll have to play me both ways (playing on both offense and defense in 6A Alabama football is not done very often, especially at a school the size of Hoover). Mom, I'm just too good to sit on the bench while the offense is on the field. It will be even better, Mom." Victor finished the statement with his trademark smile spreading from one ear to the other.

Cheryl laughed and hugged her son with pride as she told him how much she loved him. He was special, and she knew he had just done what he always did when things didn't work his way: He defused the situation and turned a negative into a positive.

What a lucky mother I am, Cheryl thought as Victor walked away. He had told her days before that he would always take care of her. If only he knew how much that was true. She couldn't imagine being so fortunate to have the wonderful children (Cortez, 12 at the time of D's death, and Syreeta, 19 at the time) she had. This child was indeed a unique young man, mature beyond his years and with a sense of wisdom most adults would pay to have.

LAST WORDS

Victor was restless that Sunday night, June 23, 2002. He was nervous about learning his new position as defensive back and concerned his summer-school class might interfere with his ability to prepare for his new position.

Cheryl noticed that he was a little agitated and restless as he went to bed, so she made a point to assure him everything would work out. She told him he would be able to take the summer-school class and still learn his new position as defensive back.

When Cheryl's alarm clock went off at 5:30 A.M. on Monday, June 24, 2002, she noticed that Victor wasn't awake. It was unusual for him to be late, and as she awakened him, she worried the stress of summer school and learning his new position might be too much. He hurried to get ready and rushed out the door after telling Cheryl he loved her.

After finishing his early morning weight-lifting workout, he left the Hoover High weight room and, at 8:00 A.M. headed to Spain Park High School for the summer school session. Cheryl went to her job as sales manager for Bell South Security Systems.

Sometime around noon, Cheryl received a phone call from the summer-school officials informing her that Victor was not going to be allowed into the Algebra 2 class. Instead of being upset, Cheryl was surprised to find that she was relieved. Now he wouldn't have the added stress of going to summer school while spending the extra hours of practice required to learn his new position.

A few minutes after 1:00 P.M., Cheryl called Victor before he began an afternoon 7-on-7 passing drill on the Hoover practice field.

"D, guess what, baby? You don't have to go to summer

school," Cheryl said.

"Mama, you're kidding! That's great! I can't believe it! I can practice with all the starters, and I won't have to miss anything." he answered.

"I love you, D."

"I love you, Mama."

PLEASE BE A DREAM

Cheryl put the phone down and was busy back at work thinking about the surprise she was going to have for Victor on his August 18th birthday: a car and a cell phone. If any 16-year-old boy deserved a car and a cell phone, it was her son.

How lucky she had been with this son. This premature miniscule baby had turned into a little man that any mother would be proud of. He was a 5'5-1/2" 163-pound ball of muscle, with an everyday smile that could light up the darkest room. He had never been sick a day in his adolescent life since overcoming his premature-baby days. Victor seemed to be on a mission to make everybody he came in touch with a better person for having known him.

Cheryl could not have been in a happier place in her life when her phone rang less than one hour after talking to Victor.

"Ms. Hill, this is Coach Matt Moore. D went down on the practice field and I think you need to come to Hoover High immediately," Coach Moore requested.

"Is he okay? What's wrong?" she asked.

"I think he is going to be fine. We're just taking precautions," Coach Moore responded.

"My God, I just talked to D. I bet he didn't eat enough. He's probably just hungry, or maybe he got too hot too fast. He's going to be okay. I just got off the phone with him," Cheryl repeated to herself as she ran to her car.

Ring, ring!

"Ms. Hill, this is Coach Moore. The EMT team is taking D to Brookwood Medical Center. Don't come to the practice field. Come straight to the hospital," Coach Moore said.

Cheryl noticed that his voice was still calm, but she could sense more concern than the first call.

"What's wrong, coach? Is D okay?"

"I think he's going to be fine. They're just taking precautions. Just meet him there," Coach Moore said, and then ended the call.

"God, let my baby be okay. Please, God, let my baby be okay. He's healthy and good. God, there isn't a better young man in this world. Let him be okay, God. Just let him be okay." Cheryl continued to pray out loud as she drove frantically to the hospital.

Ring, ring!

"Hello," Cheryl answered.

"Cheryl, Curtis just called and said D went down on the practice field and that an ambulance took him away. Is he okay?" Cassandra Dawson mother of Hoover High all-state linebacker Curtis Dawson, asked.

"I don't know, Cassandra, I don't know," Cheryl responded to her dear friend of many years.

Cheryl was speeding and dialing the Hoover Police Department simultaneously to tell them she was driving to the hospital at breakneck speeds, and for them to be aware of her arrival.

Ring, ring!

"D is gone. D is gone," Chad Jackson repeated to Cheryl. "They took him away in an ambulance. He's gone. He's gone.

They are taking him to Brookwood," Jackson said.

When Cheryl reached Highway 31, a short distance from the hospital, something hit her like a hammer. She felt her heart and her soul leave her body. It was as if the angel of death had swooped into her car and delivered the gruesome message that Victor was dead.

"Oh, no! No, God. No! Please, God, no! Don't let my baby be dead!" Cheryl prayed and begged even as she knew, if only for that moment, that her baby was dead.

She didn't want to believe it, and she continued to drive while attempting to force hope into her mind.

A few moments later, she arrived at Brookwood simultaneously to the arrival of the ambulance carrying Victor. She bolted from the car and ran toward the team of medical experts, who were working frantically to save her son.

"D! D! Let me see my baby! Let me see my baby!" she begged.

Sheppard met her before she could reach Victor and advised her to let the medical people do their job without her interference. She complied.

The team of medical life-savers rushed Victor inside without giving Cheryl a chance to touch him, to kiss him, to inhale his smell—the smell only a parent can recognize, the smell of life. She thought she was the only one who could rescue her son, but the medical team couldn't waste even a second and kept her away.

As she wandered into the hospital, reality hit her like a ton of bricks falling onto her head one at a time, each brick causing her head and her heart to shatter even more.

"I am the only one who can save my baby! Let me see my baby! Let me see my baby," she wailed, as he disappeared into the corridors of medical technology.

They took her son out of reach of the one person who truly believed she could save him, even when all the medical expertise might fail. If they would only let her love him, touch his face, and let him know she was there. Cheryl knew he would come back for her.

"This can't be real. My son left home a perfectly healthy 15-year-old young man. This can't be real. Please wake me up," Cheryl continued to murmur to herself.

Very little is clear in Cheryl's mind after that point. When they took Victor into the walls of medical science and out of the realm of family, she lost everything. She doesn't even remember her desperate charge at the hospital spokesman who guarded the door through which she could reach her son. I vividly remember her desperately lunging toward the door and swinging that haymaker overhand right—that had it landed, it would have taken Mike Tyson to his knees.

At 3:58 P.M. on June 24, 2002, a doctor from Brookwood approached Cheryl and announced, "In spite of all our efforts, we could not save your son, and he has passed."

Cheryl collapsed and remembers few details about the day from that point forward. Although she was allowed to enter into her son's room after his death, it was very little comfort, for she knew he was no longer there. His corpse lay there, frozen in time and looking as if he was only asleep. She knew he was gone long before she entered the room.

QUESTIONS? ANSWERS?

The hospital did not give Cheryl a reason for her son's death. Sure, they said he had suffered from an irregular heartbeat, or arrhythmia, but there was no explanation why. It was only a few weeks later, when she received a bill for $16,293.50 that she learned some details about what went on in the attempt to save her son. The same cruelty that refused to allow a grieving and desperate mother to hold her son in his last moments would now continue, as she looked at the bill with hopes of finding an answer for his death.

Many weeks later an official explanation of his death would be given, but not until Cheryl and her family, as well as the Hoover High football family, would endure the speculation of a community filled with rumors of drug and steroid usage, as well as some simple and healthy curiosity. No one wanted to believe a young man in perfect physical condition could just simply die. There had to be a reason.

The Internet sports-chat community and the sports talk shows would quickly fill with speculation about what really happened to Victor Hill. Nobody just dies. This was Alabama, where football was second only to God. Coaches and boosters are known to have sold their souls many times over just to find a way to win more football games.

He had to be taking something. Rumor had it the Hoover High players had been experimenting with steroids for years. How else could you explain their rapid rise to a football dynasty? It had to be more than good players and good coaching.

Cheryl, her family, and the Hoover football family would finally get their answer. Even the Hoover Police Department had entered the speculation game. According to Cheryl, she was informed the Hoover Police Department requested a second autopsy, which was done in Tennessee, to thoroughly explore any possibility of steroid use.

In the meantime, Cheryl would watch a video showing her son play his last seven plays of football for Hoover High School. A local television crew had been filming the practice session to get highlights of the All-American Jackson. There was footage of Victor lining up against his good friend and checking him one-on-one while sprinting into his defensive coverage at his new position. As she watched the video, she again realized how perfect he was until his last breath.

Victor taking steroids? No way! Everyone who knew him would never believe there was the slightest possibility of him putting a dangerous substance in his body. No, this was simply a shot at the Hoover High football program and their coaches. Victor was simply the pawn being used to play this sick game of jealousy. There were some people desperately searching for ways to hurt the Hoover program.

But that wasn't the only reason some people were asking these questions. It was also a legitimate discussion for our time, as pro athletes were under investigation for their rampant abuse of performance-enhancing drugs, and Victor, like all high school athletes, looked up to some of these so-called heroes.

Cheryl vividly remembered the phone call. It was the city of Hoover's associate coroner. Finally, thirty days after Victor's death, he had an answer. She wanted closure. Why was her son taken? There had to be a reason. She knew her son better than anyone, and she knew there was no way he would take steroids or any other drug.

But maybe, just maybe, she wondered, if only for a moment. No! She wouldn't even think of it.

"Ms. Hill, this is the City of Hoover coroner's office. I'm sorry to have to tell you this…(there was a long pause on the other end of the much anticipated phone call and Cheryl began to think maybe he had done something - maybe the temptation of trying to be the best football player had finally made him succumb to the pressure) "Ma'am, there is no explanation for your son's death. I'm sorry, but your son's body was in perfect condition. As you know, he officially died of an irregular heartbeat, but there is no reason, no explanation, as to what caused it," he finished.

"Thank you. It was simply his time," Cheryl responded somewhat relieved.

"Ma'am, you're the first person I've ever given that explanation of death to, who reacted in a voice of gratitude and not anger," the coroner said.

"You cannot explain God's work," Cheryl responded.

As she hung up the phone, she felt a slight sense of relief. Her baby had been as strong as she thought. He had never been sick, never missed school, and there was still no explanation for his death.

The doubt and questioning of the many unknowns would at least be partially over. Cheryl's spirit was temporarily lifted, and even though her struggles to understand would continue throughout her life, she had at least gained some form of closure.

My D lived the good life. No one can stain his name or his reputation, Cheryl thought, as the phone clicked and one small mystery was put to rest.

Chapter 3

Catch Amongst The Clouds

The parking lot was full two hours before kickoff. Every seat was filled with grandmas, grandpas, moms and dads, high-school students, and small children - who, though not old enough to have a clue as to what was going on, could surely feel the tension and excitement in the cool November air. College students left their Friday night parties to come home and experience this one-of-a-kind Alabama tradition of high school football playoffs.

I can "smell" football as soon as I cross the Tennessee state line on my southward journeys from Kentucky on Interstate 65. Tonight, however, was more special than usual. In my forty-plus years of playing, watching, and coaching, I had never felt the excitement, fervor, and anticipation I felt in Northport, Alabama this November 22nd night in 2002. At stake was the continued pursuit of the most coveted prize in all of Alabama football: a chance to move on to the 6A football championship game at the "Football Mecca," Legion Field, located in Birmingham, Alabama. The winner of this quarterfinal match-up would be one game closer to taking home the trophy.

The late, legendary Hall of Fame coach for the University of Alabama, Paul "Bear" Bryant, who was revered equally, if not greater, than some biblical characters by most of the population of Alabama, had to be smiling. No doubt he had the best seat in the house: that luxury suite on Heaven's 50-yard line, which had to have been built when he entered the pearly Gates of Heaven some 20-plus years ago. I guarantee, his grin spread from ear to ear as he exercised his well-earned bragging rights to a select and heavenly group of also - passed on - Hall of Fame coaching buddies. No doubt they joined him that night in his pearly-gate luxury suite.

I was somewhat jealous while soaking it all in. If only the University of Kentucky administration and boosters had paid more respect and more money to the legendary Bear in 1954, this same magical atmosphere might be in every high school in my home state of Kentucky, instead of Alabama. Well, so much for that thought, as hindsight would not change the reality of my former employer's 1954 blunder.

John Grisham couldn't have written a better script. Creating a fictional atmosphere that would come close to matching the reality of what I was soaking into my permanent memory box would be difficult for even the best of writers. Two of the state's best coaches, Robert Higginbotham of Tuscaloosa County and Rush Propst of Hoover High, were prepared to match wits for the second time in the same season. Higginbotham was a traditionalist. His philosophy was simple: Line up my eleven players against yours, coach the fundamentals of blocking and tackling and play smash-mouth, in-your-face football. Propst, on the other hand, had defied the Alabama traditionalists and made his reputation by coaching a no-huddle, fast-paced, wide-open passing attack.

The brash, cocky, and confident Propst had succeeded in doing what most old-time Alabama Hall of Fame coaches had predicted could never be done in 6A high-school football: Win, and win big, while throwing the football more than running it. It was considered a blasphemy by many old-timers, who didn't want to let go of their smash-mouth history. Many would never admit that one of their hated adversaries in college football, Steve Spurrier, formerly of the Florida Gators, who had a similar coaching style and personality of Propst's, had quite possibly cloned himself with the take-no-prisoners philosophy and brash passing attack of Propst.

It was not a surprise to anyone in the state that an overwhelming majority of high-school football fans and coaches throughout the state were pulling for the popular Higginbotham to do what no one thought possible at the beginning of the season: Beat the mighty Hoover Buccaneers' for the second time in the same season. Earlier in the season, at the Buccaneers home stadium, Higginbotham had used his team's physical style to shock the state of Alabama with a 27-24 victory over the No. 1 ranked Buccaneers.

The only thing needed to make this game any more important was a secondary story of inspiration, which had already been provided by the untimely death of Victor Hill. Movie producers should have been flying to Tuscaloosa to get the game-time scent of this traditional yet unique atmosphere.

Five minutes before the opening kickoff, I climbed a small hill on the home side of the Tuscaloosa County crowd. I was enroute to the coaches' game box (a place usually situated in the high school's press box), where strategically picked assistant coaches normally congregate to get an overhead view of the opponent. Code languages and lingo, spoken only by football coaches, is relayed through walkie-talkie headsets. Game plans, as well as the split-second adjustments, travel this radio freeway to the other coaches on the field. I was joining Hoover's quarterback coach Marty Rozell with the intention of assisting him with another set of helpful and experienced eyes. Although crowded and small, the coaches' box provided me with the perfect seat to watch a possible classic battle unfold.

God, I loved that atmosphere. There is no sporting event that matches Alabama high-school football, especially at playoff time. I'd watched high-school games in Texas, Georgia, Florida, and several other top football states, but nothing compared to the passion of Alabama high school football. If you have not allowed yourself to personally witness a game within the boundaries of this respectful and passionate State, then you've missed an important qualification required to enter the Football Fans Hall of Fame.

In Alabama, seven-year-old boys, as well as 38-year-old mothers, can tell you when a coach makes a mistake that cost his team a chance at victory. 75-year-old grandfathers can recite the top 10 plays of the season in order of their importance. Only a few school-age boys and girls will be found wandering the hot dog alleys during game time, for fear of missing a crucial play, which may be discussed in the barbershops and salons for the rest of their lives.

Simply stated, the passion for this violent yet athletic game played with oblong pigskin breeds a loyalty and reverence in Alabama communities unseen by most of the rest of the United States.

Goosebumps appeared from my head to my toes, causing a momentary shiver as I took a deep cleansing breath prior to the opening kickoff. I wanted to savor this feeling for as long as I could, with hopes I would never forget it. I wondered, with a sense of possible loss, if I would ever experience a game of this much tingling again.

THE CATCH

After exchanging scores midway through the second quarter, Hoover High was driving toward the Wildcats of Tuscaloosa County goal-line with a chance to take a commanding two-touchdown lead. The Tuscaloosa County defense was attempting to make a valiant defensive stand. Two straight defensive stops had put the Buccaneers in a third-and-goal situation from the Tuscaloosa County 17-yard line. If they could hold Hoover to a field goal attempt on fourth down, the momentum of the game would shift in their favor.

Every Tuscaloosa County fan, as well as every Hoover fan, had a strong suspicion to what play would become next. Throughout his career, All-American senior wide receiver Chad Jackson had made big play after big play. Not only did all the fans know that Jackson would probably have the pass thrown to him, but so did the Tuscaloosa County defensive players and coaches. When Jackson lined up on the right side of the field with the ball placed closer to the right hash mark than the middle of the field (high school hash marks are cut one-third of the width of the 52-yard wide fields), he was double-covered. Higginbotham had not won over 200 games as a head coach in his career by playing unsound or stupid defense. The veteran coach had decided to defend Jackson with one defender in his face and the second defender twelve yards deep, aligned almost directly on top of Jackson. The plan to double-team Jackson was a sound defensive coaching strategy.

I heard Rozell make the play call, "Ace H-orbit 619" over

his two-way radio to Propst on the sideline, and I immediately questioned him.

"Marty, I don't think you want to run that play," I said in my trademark blunt style.

"Tony, trust me, I know what I'm doing, and the play will work," Rozell responded, unflinching in his tone.

Hoover High's junior quarterback, John Parker Wilson, possessed something rare in high-school quarterbacks, as he was both football smart and book smart, eventually graduating with honors from the challenging academic environment of Hoover. As he stood with his heels five yards deep in the shotgun formation, he immediately recognized the double coverage on Jackson. He knew if he threw the ball high enough and hard enough into the back right corner of the end zone, Jackson would either come down with the ball, or at worst, make sure the Tuscaloosa County defensive backs did not intercept the pass.

Rozell relayed the call to coaches on the field who then signaled Wilson the play. The future All-American shouted the code word, and all the Hoover players looked at their 80-play wrist bands.

The play called for Jackson to line up at the Z position (football wide receiver terminology), approximately five yards from the sideline and run toward the end zone as fast as he could. The inside receiver, or the Y, as football coaches call him, would run a five-yard out route. The "X" receiver would run a slant, while the "H" and "F" would check for blitz before running check-down routes.

Evidently, there was no doubt in Wilson's mind where he was going to throw the ball as he began a short, quick-footed drop out of the shotgun formation. When he hit his last step,

Wilson fired a missile in the direction of Jackson, who was running full speed as he crossed the Tuscaloosa County goal line and headed toward the back of the end zone. Wilson had purposely thrown the football at a speed and height that made it virtually impossible for any human high-school football player, regardless of his talent, to make the catch.

Before Wilson made the throw, I quietly thought to myself, Please don't throw the ball to Jackson. He's double-covered, and this could be the turning point of the game if Hoover doesn't get a field goal (3 points) from this drive.

As I watched the ball flying through the air toward Jackson in the back of the end zone, I felt a sigh of relief. I knew Wilson had thrown the ball hard enough, and with a trajectory that no one, including Jackson, would have a chance to catch.

Sometimes when a quarterback has a tall receiver, he will throw an alley-oop type pass, where the defenders and the receiver all jump simultaneously in an attempt to out jump each other and pull down the ball as it begins its descent. This ball wasn't an alley-oop. It was traveling at a speed that showed Parker's All-American talent.

At least this pass won't be an interception, and Hoover's field-goal kicker will have a chance to increase the lead by three points, I thought.

Jackson was running in full stride, inches from the sideline, as the ball approached him five yards deep into the end zone. The ball's velocity and height made me wonder if Jackson would even make a feeble attempt to bring the ball down, or simply not waste his effort in attempting what looked to be an impossible feat.

The Tuscaloosa County safety and cornerback seemed to be thinking the same thought: *There is no way any human will catch this football, regardless of the circumstances.*

Tuscaloosa County fans and coaches seemed to relax and breathe a collective sigh of relief as they, too, watched the pass gaining velocity and climbing in altitude as it entered the area of the three players. The game was going to be a battle to the end. I have to believe that ninety-nine percent of the fans, coaches, and players all agreed, in mid-flight, that this play wasn't going to make a difference in the outcome of the game. None of the three players could touch this pass, and no one could fathom catching it.

Even though common sense led us to believe it was an impossible ball to catch, we rose to our feet and stood on our toes anyway. I now believe most of the crowd and coaches, as well as the players, subconsciously knew something special might happen, and none of us were willing to miss it. As the ball continued at breakneck speed, the rest of the crowd and I forgot one important factor: Tonight's game was not being played by mere mortals.

Jackson never changed his stride as he leapt from his left leg to attempt to catch the spiraling pass. As he rose higher into the air, I could tell his effort, though valiant, was going to be inches, if not more, short of reaching the height and distance needed to make this once-in-a-lifetime catch.

The All-American's leap had reached its ultimate height, and, from my eyes, he looked to be beginning his descent. Something strange happened that I'd never seen before and would probably never see again: Jackson began his ascent again and stretched his right arm to a height and distance only dreamed of by mere humans. It was as if he had caught his heels on a rising and speeding cloud that carried him to another level, allowing him to stretch his fingertips just high enough to touch the tight spiraling pigskin.

At the height of his ascension Jackson barely touched the ball and attempted to squeeze his fingertips around it. The crowd gasped and watched in stunned disbelief, as they knew they'd witnessed a superhuman feat performed by an 18-year-old athlete. The catch was not complete, however, as Jackson now had to land in the back of the end zone with one foot inside the out-of-bounds marker to make it a legal catch under high-school rules. With the speed and height needed to make the catch, this semi-completed feat called for an even more spectacular ending.

Jackson was now only a few feet from the landing area in the back of the end zone, and traveling at a speed that would make the inbounds landing more complicated than the catch he'd just made. To complicate the landing even more was another factor that most people watching the game never noticed. Four small boys, ages 9 to 12, had gathered in the back of the end zone to get a close-up view of this historical and spectacular attempt. The boys were standing near the back pylon (an orange marker used in the corner of the end zone to help mark the out-of-bounds area), and were within yards of the field of play where Jackson would have to land if his catch were to be ruled a legal, inbounds catch.

As Jackson began his descent, I could have sworn I saw wings open from the back of his shoulder pads and help him slow down just enough to attempt a perfect landing. I had seen the United States Army's 101st Airborne parachute specialist land with a game ball in hand on the 50-yard line on several occasions during my high-school coaching career in Kentucky, but this landing was even more athletic and precision-based than those.

Everything seemed to be moving in slow motion as Jackson's

legs began to spread as he braced for his high-speed, ballet-like landing.

Touchdown!

Touchdown!

Touchdown!

I have watched the play numerous times on video since 2002, and for the fans that haven't had the opportunity to see the play again, they probably missed his perfect landing which gracefully concluded a few feet short of those little boys in the back of the end zone.

Ironically, those four boys in the back of the Tuscaloosa County end zone happened to be Propst's two sons Jacob and Bryan, with the third and fourth culprits being his nephews Simon and John. Fifty years from now, they will sit on a porch swing and tell their grandkids a story about one of the greatest catches in the history of Alabama high-school football, and how they had the best view of any fan, or coach, in the stadium.

Hoover High players, coaches, and fans went berserk.

Jackson pranced back through the end zone, pausing only to look into the skies and give the signal that would become his trademark after every touchdown he scored the rest of his life. That signal was his respect being sent to the heavenly #8 (Victor's number), who watches Jackson play each week.

Jackson had not forgotten, that he was playing for two people: himself and his beloved cousin, the late Victor Hill.

John Parker Wilson, Marty Rozell, and Chad Jackson all knew something the rest of us momentarily forgot on that 3rd-and-17 play in Tuscaloosa County: This game was not being played by mere mortals.

Tuscaloosa County never had a chance because sitting in that luxury suite in Heaven, watching the game with the great "Bear" Bryant, was the newest member of Bryant's select group: Victor Hill.

I would love to have heard that conversation between Victor and the Bear, as the Bear most likely told Victor to run the ball and kick a field goal on fourth down. I can see Victor's trademark grin as he told the Bear to just watch his beloved "cousin" do something so spectacular that even the Bear would be impressed.

Jackson's catch wasn't human. But then again, why should it have been?

"COUSINS"

Jackson and Victor had called each other "cousin" for nearly a year. They had been friends for several years, but their bond had grown considerably in the last few months before Victor's death.

Spectacular plays were almost commonplace in Jackson's days as a Buccaneer. He would be named to numerous All-American teams after the 2002 season and would accept a football scholarship to the University of Florida. The first time I saw Jackson play was during his sophomore season. Propst had told me about this spectacular sophomore who was making plays unlike anyone he had coached before.

It was halftime of a tightly contested game (one in which the Hoover staff felt the score should be much higher in their favor) of the 2000 season, and I approached Propst in a questioning and somewhat condescending voice.

"Rush, who did you tell me your best player was?" I asked.

"Chad Jackson," he replied.

"Look at your chart and tell me how many times he's touched the football," I said.

"Give me the chart," Propst told one of his assistants.

"How many?" I sarcastically asked, knowing he had found the answer.

"Once! Before you say anything else, Franklin, I know…I'm a dumb-ass." he glared at me, his face turning red.

Propst and his assistants gathered in a circle and began to make a play script for the second half, in which Jackson would touch the ball six of the first ten plays. It didn't take long for Jackson to imprint his brilliance in my memory as he took the first play approximately 65 yards for a touchdown on a swing pass out of the back field. I knew I was watching something special, and two years later everybody in the country knew just how special a player Jackson was. What most people, including myself, didn't realize yet was just how special he was as a young man.

I met with Jackson in Hoover nearly two years after Victor's death in the spring of 2004 to discuss his relationship with his "cousin." We sat at my favorite restaurant in Birmingham, a place called *Jim N' Nicks*. We small-talked for thirty minutes or so, while stuffing our faces with barbecue, beans, and the best homemade pie in the South. After filling our faces and stomachs with a few thousand calories, we made our way back to the Hoover High parking lot where we sat for close to an hour discussing his and Victor's relationship.

"What do you remember about the catch against Tuscaloosa County?" I asked.

"Coach, when the ball left John Parker's hand, I didn't believe I had a chance of catching it. I kept running as fast as I could, and I remember that after I jumped, I thought to myself that I still had no chance of getting a hand on it. There was no one any more surprised at Tuscaloosa County than me when I was able to come down with that ball," Jackson said, with a small grin on his face. He paused and reflected for a moment before adding, "It was D, coach. I didn't make that play. He made that play. I was just the one he floated up to bring the ball down for the touchdown," he continued.

"Why did God have to take D? Jackson asked himself time and time again during our conversation.

JOURNEY TO MANHOOD

It was obvious that the All-American receiver who had just finished his first season as a Florida Gator was struggling to understand why Victor was gone. Young men in their adolescent prime shouldn't have to answer questions this difficult. Losing a dear friend is hard enough, but when you are practicing against one of your best friends, on what would be the last play of his life, and you have to stand by helplessly and watch him struggle for every breath before he dies, you have to wonder about the fairness of this game called life.

Victor had lined up for his first play as a defensive back to cover his cousin on that eventful day. A local news reporter had captured the one-on-one battle between Chad and Victor, and would later give a copy of the video to the family.

When he matched up against Chad for the first play of the 7-on-7 scrimmage, Victor seemed to be in perfect health. Jackson said there was no trash-talking from Victor; that simply wasn't his style. No, he lined up with a sheepish grin on his face as if to tell Chad, "You've met your match."

When Victor went back to the defensive huddle after the final play, Jackson said he didn't notice the collapse. It was only after several of the Hoover coaches began to loudly and firmly command him to breathe that he knew his cousin was in trouble.

"Dear God, please let D live. Let him live," Jackson remembered praying.

After they took Victor away in the ambulance, Jackson grabbed his phone and called Cheryl Hill.

D is gone. D is gone, he told her.

Jackson was driving to the hospital with fellow wide receiver Aaron Hudson.

"Don't die, D. Don't die, D. Please, God, don't let D die," Jackson prayed.

When Jackson arrived at the hospital, he witnessed several of his teammates with helpless looks on their faces. Emotions ran high, and tears began to flow freely.

I remember noticing Jackson walking with poise, seemingly calm, and with much the same demeanor he portrayed on the football field. Jackson was known for making the big play, and the catch at Tuscaloosa County would be the one that many a fan would remember him by. But his biggest catch would happen later that tragic day, before he ever entered his senior season.

The memories of June 24, 2002 aren't completely clear, but he does remember when Cheryl collapsed in total despair and shock into his arms, and he held her and comforted the mother of his fallen friend.

An 18-year-old young man had grown up more in one day than in all his previous years. Handling the death of his cousin, while maintaining his composure, was not the easiest thing Jackson had ever done. He had no choice. Not only were Cheryl and other members of her family seeking his strength but so were his teammates, who looked to him as a silent but strong leader.

Much of society tends to look at athletes as heroic and invincible characters. I sometimes find myself looking at them in their uniforms without remembering that underneath the twenty pounds of equipment is a vulnerable human being with feelings and emotions that I have sometimes ignored. At times they seem faceless.

When the doctors announced Victor's death at 3:55 P.M., Jackson was not surprised. He felt he was dead long before the announcement. Through his strong, silent, and commanding presence, the family and friends of Victor would lean on Jackson for his poise and courage.

He had just experienced the first tragedy of his young life. Later, he would openly weep with his head lying in his mother Kaye's lap, as she would try to comfort him. But June 24, 2002 was not the time for him to be seen as emotional, or even human. Jackson felt compelled to lead his teammates and a community through this unforeseen turn of events.

Jackson became a man whom I would admire regardless of his future football successes. I saw a mature man put a community and a family on his shoulders and say, "Ride me for as long as you need, for I am strong." No matter his success, or lack thereof, for the remainder of his college and possible professional career, Jackson served a purpose that will be difficult to outdo for the remainder of his life.

Nearly every top Division I football program in America offered Jackson a scholarship before his senior season. Many people, including myself, wondered how he would respond to Victor's death.

Would he be afraid?

Would he wonder if he, too, would fall and breathe his last

breath on the field?

Anyone would understand if he was apprehensive when he fell short of breath, or the humidity and heat became too intense, or if he simply was psychologically damaged to a point where his performance fell short of the record-setting history he had already achieved.

Watching Jackson in the hospital on June 24th, 2002 answered those questions for me. I had no doubt he would overcome any challenges that football, or eventually life, would set in front of him.

FEAR

The heat in late July and early August in Alabama can be, and usually is, stifling and smothering, to say the least.

Two weeks following Victor's death, the Buccaneers were back beginning workouts and preparing for a national 7-on-7 passing tournament, which would be hosted by Hoover High. The best football teams in the south, east, and northeast had entered this one-of-a-kind prestigious passing tournament, and the Buccaneer coaches would get an opportunity to see how their players responded to adversity, sweltering heat, humidity, and psychological trauma.

Would they compete? Would they be mentally "down"? Would they be afraid, back off, and not push themselves when the heat and humidity became unbearable?

Hoover entered the tournament as one of the favorites, but after finishing the qualifying rounds with a 4-4 record, they found themselves barely making it into the playoff round. Evangel Christian, from Shreveport, Louisiana, who had the No. 1 quarterback in the nation (John David Booty, who would eventually play for Southern California) thoroughly drubbed

Hoover by more than four touchdowns in one of the tournament's qualifying games.

Jackson had been merely average in his performances during the eight games.

"Tony, do you think our coaches are laying off our players? You know what I mean...taking it easy on them from their own fear from Victor's tragedy," Propst asked me before they entered the playoffs.

"Not really. But I certainly couldn't blame them if they are," I answered.

"I think they are, and I believe the players are timid. If I don't get them out of this, it could carry on into the season, and we could really be in trouble," Propst told me.

He walked away, with a purposeful stride I had seen once before. I knew what was coming next. The young men from Hoover High School were about to receive a classic ass-chewing, of a style and tenacity that few coaches have the ability to pull off.

All the players' eyes were fixed on Propst as he loudly and convincingly reminded them that the game of football required intensity, emotion and precision. The Buccaneers were showing none of these characteristics. Propst didn't spare his assistant coaches from his tongue lashing either, and when he was finished, the entire football team—players and coaches—walked away with the much needed, although somewhat temporary, ferocity to compete in the tournament.

Propst, as usual, had read his players emotions perfectly. They responded with three straight victories and a trip to the championship game, a rematch with Evangel Christian.

The temperature was nearing 100 degrees, and the humidity seemed to be worse. This would be a challenge to see how the

Buccaneer players, and especially Jackson, would respond in the potentially dangerous weather conditions.

Early in the game, Hoover fell behind two touchdowns and it seemed as if Evangel would repeat the thrashing they had given them earlier in the tournament. Evangel was simply too good. Booty appeared to be every bit as good as advertised, and the rest of the cast for Evangel was more than proficient.

Propst decided the only chance Hoover had would be if he turned up the tempo and went into their Nascar system, which forced both teams to play at a pace two to three times faster than normal. He also decided Jackson would play offense and defense.

After making a spectacular catch in the end zone for a touchdown to cut the lead back to one score, Jackson began to walk toward the sideline. The closer he got, the dizzier he felt.

No, No, God. Not me, too, Jackson thought, as his overheated body and brain tricked him into a helpless feeling. He was sure a collapse was inevitable.

Jackson felt himself slump to both knees as he put his hands on the ground in front of him. His mind continued to play tricks as he struggled to execute a deep cleansing breath.

Could it be happening to me? Surely not. God, not like D, the fear rushed through Jackson's brain.

As Jackson stayed on the ground for a few seconds and labored to breathe, he suddenly remembered his mother was sitting in the stands. She must be terrified to see him on his knees, laboring for his next breath. He gathered energy from some unknown source and bolted upwards, landing on his feet, and immediately sprinted back onto the field with renewed breath and spirit.

From that moment forward, he would never worry about

dying on the field again.

Jackson made several spectacular catches, as well as defensive plays, in a double-overtime loss to Evangel. He had gained a power and divine strength that would carry him through his senior season, and probably through the remainder of his career. No more fear was hidden in his subconscious, at least not the fear of dying on a football field.

#8 GOES TO COLLEGE

Jackson gained an angel when he lost his cousin. He still doesn't understand why God chose to take Victor when He did, but he understands that Victor loved the game of football so much that no matter how hot, how tough the challenge, or how good the opponent, Jackson would always have an extra edge: Victor would be there to help him.

Victor had been there to help him catch Cheryl as she collapsed and fell in the hospital. He had been there to help him climb on top of the clouds to wrap his fingertips around the football at Tuscaloosa County, and he had helped provide the wings that allowed him to safely land inbounds while avoiding Propst's sons and nephews in the end zone. He he had been there when Jackson went to his knees in the sweltering heat in late July against Evangel - only weeks after his death—to tell him, "It's okay, get up and go play!"

He would go with Jackson to Florida to help him compete against the nation's top players every day in practice, and on Saturdays on national television.

Most players and coaches know when you wear the #1 jersey on the football field, you are asking for every player on the opposing team to take an extra shot at you. They believe you have chosen to wear #1 because of your ego and your belief that you are the best player on the field. Jackson was known throughout the country as #1. He wore the number with spectacular results, as his statistics told the rest of the world he was something special, someone who deserved to wear that number. He was more than willing to become the opponent's bull's-eye.

When Victor died, Jackson went to Propst to talk to him about wearing his number.

"I want to wear D's #8 in memory of him," Jackson told Propst.

"Chad, you've spent your entire career establishing the #1 as your trademark and your identity. I understand you wanting to respect D and honor him by wearing his number, but I want you to maintain your identity. But, I'll compromise with you," Propst responded. "I'll let you wear the #8 for the first game of the season to honor Victor in a professional and classy method. The rest of the season you'll continue to wear #1, but I'll make one exception. I'll let you wear #8 the last game of the season. You know what the last game of the season is, don't you?" Propst probed Jackson.

"Yes, sir. The last game of the season is the state championship game at Legion Field," Jackson said, as he walked away with a confident smirk, knowing he would be wearing the #8 in the two most important games of his senior season.

After the opening game ceremonies to honor Victor, neither Propst or Jackson mentioned the #8 again until the week of the state championship game. Number 8 would catch seven passes for 145 yards and three touchdowns in Hoover's victory over Montgomery Jeff Davis in the 2002 6A State Championship game at Legion Field. Number 8 would also throw a new state-championship record 80-yard touchdown pass.

Number 8 had always dreamed about being the star in the

state championship game. He was! Heaven and Earth teamed up to make #8's dreams come true.

I can see Victor sitting in that luxury box again with the great Bear Bryant sitting beside him and discussing whether Hoover was throwing the ball too much in the state championship game. The Bear probably let Victor get the best of him that day, in at least that one heavenly conversation. Besides, it was a day especially set aside for #8. How could the Bear argue with that?

When the equipment manager at the University of Florida passed out jerseys for the new incoming freshman in the fall of 2003, Jackson requested the number that had become number one in his heart: the #8.

Victor desperately wanted to play college football, probably as much as anyone who ever played the game. On each Saturday that Jackson lines up for the University of Florida, #8 is living his dream.

Jackson scored his first college touchdown against San Jose State in Gainesville, Florida in front of more than 90,000 screaming Gator fans. When he reached the end zone, he stopped and pointed a finger toward the heavens and made a signal to the #8.

Victor is still playing!

Chapter 4

Dying For Victory

THE LOOGIE LESSON

Natalie can't spit these days without a slight grin appearing. Each time the urge to launch a big loogie compels her, she imagines Victor floating in the clouds and rolling with his infectious laughter, as well as sticking out his chest with the pride of a good teacher. She knows he is laughing with her, not at her - that was his style.

Very few coaches or athletes in this world have been able to master this art for themselves, and only a few are willing to teach it. If you want to be your best as an athlete you must master the art of successfully launching a loogie during competition, without losing an edge. To the non-athlete this may seem a simple task, but athletes will tell you the process of exiting a loogie from the back of the throat without losing a step can be complicated during a competitive event. This unnatural skill of spitting while competing might be the difference in winning and losing. A discombobulated effort to launch the unwanted saliva from the body could cause you to lose a precious second.

It was Valentine's Day, 2005, and former Hoover athlete

Natalie Boone was in the second semester of her freshman year at the University of Alabama. From the moment she answered the phone I was enthralled by her unusual charm, personality, and wit. She was a former Hoover High volleyball player, known for her competitive spirit, who graduated in May of 2004.

With a deep laugh, she recalled that memorable day in the sixth grade at Simmons Middle School when her loogie coach, Victor, gave her a concise, step-by-step instruction and demonstration of how to forcibly launch a loogie. He executed, with the precision of an experienced marksman, a perfectly launched loogie that sailed far away from his body, never touching his skin or clothes.

She couldn't wait for the first opportunity to practice her new method of loogie launching. The hilarious part of the lesson was the serious nature in which Victor explained, and she listened. Another belly laugh surged from her as she reminded me of the laser-like focus she had demonstrated during this spitting lesson as a sixth-grade athlete in search of an edge. This was serious business.

Victor and Natalie's PE teacher set up a competition for the mile run. Natalie had two major goals: (1) beat Victor in the mile run, (2) demonstrate her newfound ability to blast a perfectly launched loogie. The loogie must travel far enough from her body to have no saliva remains clinging to her, which would be extremely humiliating and embarrassing.

Early in the race, it became evident that Natalie's mission of beating Victor wasn't going to happen. However, halfway around her first lap, she felt the urge to spit.

Stay focused, hock it up from the throat, and aim clearly away from the body, she recited in her mind. *Spit with such force, there is no chance this gross projectile will land anywhere* near you, she mentally rehearsed.

As she gathered all of her strength and mustered the courage to spit the loogie, she thought to herself, *Just do it girl,* and let it fly. The result: A huge glob of saliva successfully left her mouth, but the speed and aim were slightly off, and it missed its intended land target. Instead, it found a nearby landing spot on her right arm.

She had failed miserably and was embarrassed, not so much for the huge loogie on her arm, but because she had failed to learn from Victor's valuable spitting lesson. She finished the mile without ever wiping the loogie off her arm for fear that someone, especially Victor, would see her. Natalie had failed in one of Victor's most hilarious lessons.

In August of 2002, two months after Victor's passing, Natalie began writing a lighthearted poem about the loogie lesson. Unable to finish the poem, it sat untouched until her senior year, when she began to study *Macbeth* and the inevitability of death. The reflection had started as simple and fun, but evolved into an introspective view of the small things in life we take for granted.

Loogie

At first I think it is a rumor…
You know how people exaggerate.
But then I get three more phone calls
Abominable signs.

While driving to the church I think of the days
when coming in before dark
and being the loudest at pep rallies
was most important on our minds.
How did I let this childish charisma mature too soon?

I loved our youth.
In PE class you challenged me every day.
The only thing I ever beat you at was the V-sit,
but we were young and carefree
and soaked up the vivacity of life.
Now every time I spit I think of you.
I remember how you taught me during Coach Bank's class.
The first time I tried I failed miserably
but you laughed
and I laughed.
Something that was so childish and seemingly insignificant,
became pivotal when you fell the same place you played.
Your playfulness allowed me to see
that everything is significant…
even loogies.

You were a brief candle
and then out out…
but you taught me how small things
signify everything.

UNDER THE RADAR

After moving to Hoover from Prattville, Alabama in the sixth grade, Natalie immediately struck up a friendship with Victor. She remembered sitting in a class feeling lonely and wondering if she would ever make a friend, when Victor came bouncing into her world in the summer of 1997. Her life would never be the same. Over the five years Natalie watched Victor make several lonely or out-of-place students feel comfortable and accepted. They would become close friends over the next five years and would talk or exchange text messages on a daily basis until the day he died.

When I asked Natalie why she and Victor had become such good friends, she laughed and said, "When we first met, D had a crush on me, and I never let him forget it. There was chemistry between us, partially because we were both so competitive. Neither one of us would accept losing. In our sixth grade PE class at Simmons Middle School, it seemed like every time the teams were chosen, we were on opposite sides competing against each other. Both of us were so competitive we would scratch the other one's eyes out to win."

"I know D respected me as a competitor, and I certainly respected him."

"Most of us were drawn to D because of his simplicity. He would walk into a room and instantly make us relaxed and comfortable. He was one of the few people I've known who chose friends based not on what they could do for him, but what he could do for them."

"His friends ranged from athletes to geeks, from young to old, from male to female, and from jocks to the band members. There wasn't a person born that D didn't find something in their character to like."

"He taught me to see life with no constraints. He made us all laugh, but he still seemed to fly under the radar. His philosophy of life attempted to call out and say, 'I'm in this world for only a short time, and I'm going to make the best of it, not just for me, but for every human I come in contact with,'" Natalie sighed, and paused for a moment.

"After reading Lisa Beamer's book *Let's Roll!*, which told the story of the tragic 9-11 plane crashes and the role Lisa's husband, the late and heroic Todd Beamer, played, I was reminded of other reasons why D was so special. In the book, Lisa shared her memories of Todd being a man that was loved by most everyone and had very few, if any, enemies. His motto was, 'Fly beneath the radar'.

"*Let's Roll!* reminded me how D lived his life. Even in the sixth grade, when D was the big man on campus because of his athletic stardom, he was unusually humble, a characteristic my parents had emphasized to me since I was a small child as one of the most import qualities any human can have. When he had a chance to utilize his big-man-on-campus persona for personal glory, he simply chose to fly beneath the radar. Daily, he would enter a classroom and seek out an unknown or shy student, and find a way to make them feel part of the group. After bringing a smile to their face, he would walk away ever so quietly, under the radar, until the next time they needed someone to pick them up and make them laugh."

"D seemed to have it all: He was liked by girls, a great athlete, yet extremely humble and always open to listen to someone who might be able to help him improve in any area of life."

"Learning from D continued for me even after his death. I was 16 at the time and had never been to a funeral for anyone outside of my Caucasian background. I remember the uniqueness of being at my first funeral for a group of people other than my own race, in this case an African American who happened to be one of my closest friends. The sadness and crying were prevalent, just as they had been in the other funerals I had attended, but what stuck in my memory were the joy and happiness, as well as a spiritual acceptance of an horrific event that seemed to say, 'Tragedy happened-now deal with it'.

"An open microphone was available for anyone in the room to come forward and share memories about D. A poem was read and a joyful song was performed by a duet. I realized, through this unique celebration of his life, he was still teaching me, even after his death. A new perspective about life and friends emerged, especially the circle of life, and how it is supposed to be lived.

That image is permanently embedded in my memory."

Natalie loves Victor. She loves to recount the text messages he sent her every day, and the fact that he genuinely cared about her, just as he cared about everyone he came in contact with. She loved him because his giving to others was an everyday occurrence, not something he did in order to draw attention to himself. She loved him because he moved her to a mature stage in life that she might never have reached had it not been for his lesson, the lesson of living every day as if it might be your last.

On Victor's last day on this earth, Natalie hadn't taken the time to return Victor's daily text message. Today, she never puts off any deed for friends because she understands that life is the one thing you can't take for granted. Victor taught her that through his life and his death.

"He taught me to live life with no constraints and to be friends with everyone, regardless of their sex, race, or background. I was in awe of his life," Natalie concluded.

YOUR GAME - MY GAME

V is for Victory-Carry on Buccaneers! Go! I is for Impossible-to beat our team, you know! C is for Coach-who helped us lead the way. T is for Touchdown-that's us every single play. O is for Orange and black-the colors of the best. R is for Renewal-you and me one day...God bless!

Hoover schoolmate Ali Patton provided me with this poem Victor had written months before his death. With each letter in his name, he signaled a positive outcome for his beloved Buccaneers. Unlike most male athletes, including myself, he was secure enough in his masculinity that he actually read it aloud to some of his teammates prior to his death. It was as if he had a sixth sense of things to come. He eventually shared the poem, as well as his feelings of camaraderie with all the Hoover athletes—men and women. The poem still hangs in Coach Propst's office today.

Prior to each ladies basketball game, Lady Buccaneer Jordan Gann could expect to see her same favorite visitor hanging around to wish her and the team good luck. Many times football players, afraid of challenging their masculinity, can't find the time, or self-confidence, to loudly support a girl's basketball team. Victor was different, of course. He saw the Hoover girls basketball team as being just as important as the football team, and he made a point to let each one of the girls know he would be there yelling for them and expecting them to pull out the victory.

Whether it was a cold spring day, or one of sweltering summer heat, each team could expect to have at least one fan in the stands or on the fence row, yelling and screaming as if it were the last game they would ever play. Victor was the biggest fan, with the most school spirit for each sport, whether it was the men's baseball team or the ladies' softball team. He used his school spirit and never-ending energy to make the game fun.

MY BEST FRIEND

"Coach, when I first moved to Hoover from Nashville at age 14, I was afraid I would never again have a really close friend. I had lived in Nashville all my life, and my cousins and other family were everywhere. Sure, I had pals, but I just knew that no one would ever be as close to me as my cousins and family. My nervousness ended the day I met D," former Hoover offensive lineman and teammate Deontai Clemmons recalled.

Clemmons, who was preparing to begin his pre-med studies

at the University of Alabama, had entered the Barnes & Noble bookstore somewhat shy and slightly trembling. I knew many of the Hoover running backs, wide receivers, and quarterbacks very well, but since I didn't work with the offensive linemen or defensive players, they were not as comfortable or open at the beginning of our conversation. I could tell he was struggling to talk about Victor's death, as his voice began to crack, so I asked him about his life.

"He shared his dreams with me of one day becoming the next Warrick Dunn (former Florida State and current Atlanta Falcon star running back, whose diminutive size was comparable to Victor's), and in the next breath he wanted to know what my dreams were. Instantly, he would change his thought process and spend the remaining part of a conversation focusing on you achieving your dreams, not him achieving his," Clemmons recalled, with his face and tone showing a pride similar to that of a parent espousing the accomplishments of their children.

"We both were born with the name Deontai, my first name and his middle name, even though we spelled it differently. Within minutes of meeting him I knew I was going to fit in at Hoover. D made sure of it. I had this instant premonition that he was my best friend."

"Coach, how many people have told you that D was their best friend?"

"Several," I responded.

Laughing deeply, Clemmons continued, "You see, coach, everybody who knew D thought he was their best friend. That was one of his greatest gifts. I promise you, there were at least 200 people at his funeral who would swear to you that D was their best friend. And they might have been right - he was capable of having hundreds of friends and keeping them all happy.

How many people can do that?"

Another close friend of Victor's, David Jones, shared a similar analogy. "We had many memorable moments, going back to the sixth grade when we met, including D's hilarious attempt to become a blonde during our spring break trip to Panama City in 2001. All those memories were flooding my brain as I walked down the long aisle of Hunter Street Baptist Church, carrying his body as one of the pallbearers. I looked into the crowd of more than a thousand mourners and was instantly overcome with emotion when I realized (just as Clemmons had) that my best friend was indeed everyone's best friend."

FLAWLESS

"Flawless! He had no enemies. A polite, great guy. I can't think of one single negative to associate with D's name," Kristen Smith, a freshman at the University of Alabama-Birmingham, relayed to me on Valentine's Day, 2005 during our phone conversation.

She related a story about the times Victor would sneak into the theater class prior to its beginning, just to make sure everyone was happy and having a good time.

"The theater teacher would tell D, in a lighthearted attempt to scold him, to hurry on to his next class. He felt like he was everybody's guardian angel and it was his job to make sure everyone was having a good time. He possessed a charisma only a few people are blessed with," Smith recalled.

"D had recently moved closer to my house, and there were many days he would ride by, even occasionally sneaking a quick underage practice drive in his mom's car, just to say hello. My mother loved D as much as anyone and was devastated by his death. There were no age limits for his spirit of good will to touch you, as my mother can attest. She was mesmerized by his spirit and gusto for life, and couldn't wait for him to drop in. We had begun planning weekly car wash sessions to start when he got his driver's license."

"I couldn't get enough of his life. He made me realize what it was like to never be in a bad mood. He was an awesome life teacher," Smith said.

"Look, I'm in two places at the same time!" Victor shouted to his friend and classmate Kendra Reynolds.

He was straddling one foot in each county, the Jefferson County and Shelby County boundary line, and Kendra was soaking in his joy for life. His exuberance with each small detail of life took her breath away. Whatever happened in a given day, Victor would put it in a unique perspective, leaving her in adulation of his insatiable thirst for living.

Kendra reflects back and is still astonished at his devotion to other people. "I saw his limitless spirit and his ability to always achieve, even from the most unlikely of circumstances," she remembers.

"He had a commitment to friends that was constantly in force. One day, after talking on the phone to a friend of mine and discovering she was at my house—two miles from his—he appeared at the doorstep in less than thirty minutes simply to say hello and brighten our day. He walked!"

"I aspire to follow his example today and be the kind of friend he was. His simple acts of daily kindness and devotion inspire me to honor my commitment to friends," Kendra wrote in a note describing their relationship.

"D's presence was inspirational during my tough times in sports. I would be shivering on a cold blustery day on the softball field, wondering if any classmates would show up to watch our game, and suddenly, out of nowhere, he would appear yelling for my team and me."

"His life was more than influential - it was unmatchable and incomparable to anyone I have known. There is no substitution for D's life. His existence and the legacy he left are indeed rare," Kendra finished, closing her reflection of her unique friend.

PLAY EVERY PLAY

Victor's 7th-and 8th-grade football teams won only one game combined. Players in all sports sometimes quit competing or constantly complain, if the team isn't winning or if they aren't making any plays to give themselves recognition. It is a normal, and almost expected, reaction of young and old people alike to struggle to give maximum effort when things don't go right in life or in sports.

Wayne Wood has spent more than twenty-six years as a teacher and coach for middle schools in Alabama. He has seen every type of family situation and excuse for life's problems. He has also coached many special players who have gone on to achieve greatness in sports and life. But one memory sticks out as much as any championship or spectacular play he has ever coached or witnessed.

"We (Simmons Middle School) were playing Thompson Middle School at the Hoover High Stadium. They were leading us by a large margin late in the fourth quarter, with no chance for us to come back and win. There were only a few seconds left, and our kids were driving for a consolation touchdown. We threw an interception, and one of their biggest and fastest players was running for an uncontested touchdown to make the margin of the score even worse. He was 10-15 yards in front of everyone, and no one had a chance at catching him," Wood recalled with the details only a coach can remember.

"This poor group of kids was going to have another negative memory to take with them from their middle-school football careers."

"Out of nowhere, flying at warp speed, comes Victor. He is gaining ground, stride by stride, and eventually shocks the remaining crowd when he catches the startled player. He is a big kid and a great athlete, and Victor has to ride his back like a cowboy on the rodeo circuit. The Thompson player keeps fighting, yard after yard, but he's no match as Victor pulls him to the ground a few feet short of the end zone. Victor jumped up and stood triumphantly over him. He was a winner," Wood said, with his voice cracking as the tears floated slowly down the lines of his broken face.

"Play each play as hard as you can. You never know when it might be your last one!"

This phrase is a common motivational ploy used by coaches for decades. Although coaches preach this intensity at every level of competition, few athletes truly understand and compete at that level. Victor was one of those few.

ON THE EDGE

"He was fun-loving and crazy, living on the edge and never taking a single day for granted!" former Hoover running back and current Samford University defensive back B. T. Hartloge exclaimed.

"I'll never forget the day he dyed his hair blond just to see what he would look like. He had no limits on what he'd do to make any day special. We used to go to the bluffs (an area on a local lake with 30-40 foot cliffs), and he would dive forty feet into the water with no fear. Exploring his limitations seemed to be a daily destiny. I don't believe he was afraid of anything, especially death," Hartloge recalled June 5, 2004, in a conversation at the Barnes & Noble bookstore at the Summit Mall in Mountain Brook.

"We played the same position, and I knew he was as good, if not better, than me, but when it came time to sacrifice for the good of the team and move to defense, D did it with the best attitude anyone could have displayed. Hoover football meant everything to him, and sacrificing for the good of the team was second nature for him.

The one thing that always amazed me was that D never got tired. He could run forever. I was never in the best condition I could have been, but he could have run the entire practice or game without stopping.

It just doesn't make sense - him dying the way he did.

"He was such a phenomenal leader, by example and with his mouth. If you slacked off in practice, he might jump down your throat. A lot of guys couldn't get away with that, but he did because he outworked all of us. A minute after chewing us out, he would slap us on the butt with a big grin on his face, telling us we could make it.

He taught me how to overcome adversity. And he taught me to make a positive out of all negatives. Every time I get tired today I think of him and find a way to push myself harder. My desire and passion for life is double because I knew him.

"Coach, I still keep in my bedroom the list of rules you gave me to be a great running back. Victor and I shared them, and he wrote them down for me. They are in his handwriting, and I'll never lose them."

"Do you think D knew he was going to die?" Hartloge asked, with a slightly puzzled look as we finished our conversation.

"Why do you ask?" I responded.

"Because he lived like there was no tomorrow," Hartloge said, as we shook hands and he walked away.

PEANUT BUTTER OR STEAK

Former Hoover teammate and offensive lineman Cliff Groce still wears a necklace with the #8 dangling from his neck as he continues his football career at Huntingdon College. He, along with his younger sister Mallory, was one of Victor's close friends. It only seemed natural for their mother Tammy to want to comfort Cheryl when the tragedy happened.

But Tammy had her own reasons for joining other mothers to comfort and assist Victor's family. She joined Beth Hartloge, Julie McCain, Cassandra Dawson, and other moms who sometimes spent sleepless nights and never ending days with Cheryl. They held her and comforted her in their arms in ill-fated attempts to help her garner one moment of non-nightmarish sleep. Tammy loved Victor too. Both her children had been blessed when Victor became their friend, but Tammy had received the same blessing when she casually observed his interaction with her children, as well as herself.

"He loved life," she told me at the Courtyard Marriot lobby in Hoover on June 5, 2004, about one hour before I would interview her son. "It was written all over his face!"

"I fed him meals at the house with Cliff and Mallory, and his face lit up when it was a peanut butter sandwich, just as much as it did when it was a steak. He was truly grateful - not just kissing up to some mom who might give him another good meal one day."

"D was a part of our family, but his unique gift was that he was a part of everyone's family. Not only did he make himself feel at home in your house, he made you feel as if he was one of yours."

"I was in awe of how much he wanted everyone to succeed. He cared so much that you couldn't help but love him."

As the tears began to stream down her beautiful Alabama face, she recalled how much it hurt her to see her son and daughter have their hearts ripped apart by Victor's tragedy.

"After going to Hunter Street Baptist Church and watching these massive, macho, muscle-ripped football players, as well as their coaches, crumble- with their souls struggling for answers—I knew I had to go help Cheryl.

"The moment I entered the door, she walked toward me and collapsed into my arms. She had been hugged and loved on by everyone she knew for the last several hours, and I knew she needed more than that from me.

"For the next three weeks, several of us moms, as well as her family, tried to be her servant- whether it was cleaning house, assisting with meals, organizing her day, or simply holding her at night while she cried herself to sleep.

"D brought love, respect, unrestricted friendship, and laughter into my home for me and my children. He taught me that love and friendship are not restricted by race, economics, or unimportant differences. When it was time for me to demonstrate what I had learned from him, I was thankful that Cheryl allowed me and the other mothers to be her comfort and servant for a time in her life when she desperately needed it," Tammy concluded, as she wiped the tears from her mascara-dampened face.

JON AND JON

With a scrubby beard, earrings, an eyebrow ring, and tattoos, the two young men walking toward me were hard not to notice. Cheryl had had a mischievous smile on her face earlier in the day, as she told me how enlightening these two friends of Victor would be. Surely this couldn't be who she was talking about, I thought to myself as they approached my table. They didn't fit the physical descriptions of the other young men I had been interviewing.

I had spent the last three days talking with numerous coaches, players, and parents - interviewing them at the Barnes & Noble bookstore, the Courtyard Marriott, and in their homes. The football players were almost statuesque in their definitively muscled bodies. Hoover is a wealthy school district and many of the players come from upper-middle-class or above backgrounds. Combined with the tough discipline and successful weight lifting program required to be a Hoover football player, the young people I had previously interviewed were seemingly perfect in looks and stature.

These two young men didn't look the part. They were frail and fragile compared to the others I had interviewed so far. My mind began to wander as I tried to guess what Victor would have in common with them.

I never had a real true friend until the sixth grade, when I met D. For some reason, I just didn't connect with people," Jonathan McCain said, as he slumped in the hotel lobby chair.

His eyebrow ring was speaking to me about Victor's outreach as loudly as his words as he continued, "I played football just to hang around him. I was in no way a very good player, mostly a second-team guy on a bad middle-school team, but D taught me to compete just as hard as the starters. He would push me to be my best, and I would push him in return.

"When I quit playing football in the 9th grade, D was upset

because we didn't have as much time together, but he was really upset because I began to drift away from doing the right thing in my daily living. I had begun to get into trouble and was close to making some serious mistakes in my life. D was so distraught about my poor decisions that he actually broke down and cried once because some of his friends were talking bad about me. It hurt him worse than if they had been talking bad about him. Some of my old friends disassociated themselves from me. I don't blame them, but thank God D never gave up on me," McCain reflected, as he gazed away.

"One day this guy tried to start a fight with D for no reason, other than to just start trouble. By the time D finished talking his anger down, he had the guy bent over laughing. His personality was magnetic, and his ability to sincerely care for everyone he came in contact with was a rare gift.

"I was like McCain: shy, reserved, and didn't have many friends," a scraggly bearded Jon Dunham interjected into the conversation."

Dunham has a tattoo on his back in memory of Victor. He explained the reasoning and details of the tattoo. "First off, I designed it myself, and actually drew the entire thing out. I put a lot of thought into it. It's a cross with a D in the middle and the sun behind it. And underneath it an the words, '*Gone But Not Forgotten.*'

"The cross shows D's strong faith and religious beliefs, as well as mine, and the belief that we will meet again. The "D" is obvious. It shows that the tattoo is for him. '*Gone But Not Forgotten*' because we will never forget him. The sun represents the fact that he was a strong light in my life, as well as everyone he came in contact with," Dunham continued.

"The other question I get is, 'Why on your back?' Well, even the placement has meaning to me. D was always there looking out for me. He had my back. The cross is located on my left shoulder blade, close to where my heart is in my chest, as a representation that he will always be close to my heart and always looking over my shoulder," Dunham said.

"I decided to play football at Simmons Middle School in the 6th grade and D puts me under his wing and breaks me out of my shell. We remained weight-room workout buddies until I quit playing in the 10th grade.

"After I quit playing, we stayed friends because once you were his friend, you were always his friend. He was like a guardian angel to McCain and me. We both occasionally needed someone to look us in the eye and tell us to get back on the right path. D did it without judgment. He was so much more than a football player.

"You've probably heard all kinds of football stories about D and they're all fun and true, but McCain and I watched D do things that some of his teammates would have thought him crazy for doing. We used to walk four miles to Lake Cyrus. There were these cliffs, thirty to forty feet high, which we would jump off of into the water. He would turn flips and occasionally do this dive we named 'the flying squirrel,' where he would reach back in mid-air and grab his ankles, spreading his body wide, then, just before contact, he would attempt to turn it into a perfect dive.

"He was totally fearless," Dunham continued, his grin disappearing as he seemed suddenly distracted.

"The past couple of months before he died, he seemed to be spending more time at home with his family. It was strange. I actually hadn't seen him for more than two weeks before his tragedy," he said.

"Do you know about his bible?" Dunham quizzed me.

"No. What about it?" I responded.

"You need to read his bible. He had just begun underlining these verses. I'm not going to tell you about them, except to say that he may have had a premonition about things to come," Dunham said, as he and McCain shook my hand and headed out the door.

My curiosity was gnawing at me as they left. I couldn't wait to talk to Cheryl and see what they were referring to in his bible.

As with all the young people I had interviewed before them, both Dunham and McCain loved Victor. But I sensed there was something different about their feelings - something much stronger than the others.

It's been almost three years now since Victor died and my premonition about Dunham and McCain was true. As everyone moved on in their lives and the phone calls and impromptu visits to Cheryl eventually stopped, three men kept the promises they'd made at an emotional time to their deceased friend: McCain, Dunham, and David Jones.

Whenever Cheryl feels herself spinning into an emotional depression, Dunham, McCain, or Jones will show up unannounced at her doorstep, similar to the friendly tone of an AOL instant message arriving at your computer. One of the three will always find a way to put a smile on her face.

You see, they have never forgotten the life lesson their friend Victor gave them. He was always there for them, even when it wasn't cool to be their friend. Cheryl knows that as life passes by, and her struggles to deal with the loss of her son continue, she will always have these men to remind her of the incredible difference he made in the short time he was here on this earth.

Chapter 5

The Trainer

FIX ME "DOC"

The worst job in all of sports has to be the somewhat thankless job of the athletic trainer. Each day, athletes walk into their office and complain that some part of the body isn't working right and is in pain. It is the trainer's job to diagnose their injury, heal it, and then play psychologist and make them believe it was never hurt to begin with. If they show too much empathy and compassion, some of the players will use it against them in an attempt to find an excuse to miss a practice or rehab session.

In the meantime, the head football coach will walk in, look the trainer in the eye, and ask one question, "When will you have him ready to play?" His job and reputation depends on how fast he is able to get players back on the field playing near the 100% performance level.

"DOC"

The first trainer I knew made a lasting impression on me, as well as most of my teammates. Tom "Doc" Simmons was the athletic trainer at Murray State University in 1976, when I enrolled as a freshman to play football. My first impression of Doc was a hard-nosed, uncompassionate, horse's ass. He seemed gruff, rude, and short with everyone he came in contact with. The training room was the last place any player wanted to find himself. It took me a few years as a high-school coach to realize he was doing exactly what he was supposed to do: He was forcing players to realize their job was on the field performing, not lounging in the training room believing they were injured.

A trainer has to develop the demeanor of a businesslike, gruff miracle worker. "Fix me, Doc" is the universally spoken, and unspoken, cry of athletes immediately after an injury occurs. The athlete glazes into the trainer's eyes and anticipates him performing some type of miracle to get him back on the field without missing many plays. The best trainers will make a player understand the difference between pain (it hurts but still works well enough to perform) and injury (it doesn't function well enough to perform).

One of the trainer's most difficult jobs is bringing a player through physical rehabilitation over a grueling six-month or longer period. He must demand more from the player than the player actually believes he has, and then guide the athlete through this pain threshold into an era of recovery that, if successful, cumulates with the player having faith that he is better than he was before the injury.

In November, 1976, I realized firsthand that Doc had caring and compassion hidden beneath his gruff exterior.

It was near the end of the second quarter when I stumbled over my own clumsy feet while attempting to blast my way into the end zone. I was somewhere near the five-yard line stripe on the concrete-like Astroturf of the Austin Peay State University football field in Clarksville, Tennessee. My wrist and elbow hit the turf simultaneously, and the bones shattered immediately. I took myself out of the game and slowly trotted to the sideline with my shattered right arm cradled in my left hand. The intense pain combined with my inability to move my fingers or arm led me to believe this wasn't a common tough-it-out injury and that something was seriously wrong.

Earlier that season, in my first career start against Morehead State University, I had caught a pass and had both pinkies dislocate upon contact from a vicious hit by the free safety. I was withering in pain as Doc grabbed each pinkie and jerked it back into place. I missed one play, and then went back in and finished the game. That was pain- but not an injury- as my body still functioned well enough to perform.

This time was different. Doc walked over to me and asked if I was ready to go back in, to which I immediately replied no. The look in his eyes led me to believe that he also knew, even though no bones were sticking out of the skin, that something was definitely malfunctioning. It was serious enough to request our team doctor, Hal Houston, to evaluate the injury. They both agreed to wait until halftime to further evaluate the seriousness of my now slightly deformed-looking and rapidly swelling right arm.

I was known for being a tough, hardnosed, straight ahead runner (which, at 185 pounds, basically meant that I was too slow to outrun anyone and had no evasive moves to make a tackler miss me in open space). The truth was, I didn't play very well with pain. I'm man enough to admit it today. It's probably one of the reasons I consider myself too soft to be a great head coach, as I have way too much empathy for players when I think they're hurt.

One thing was for certain as I entered the Austin Peay

locker room a few minutes prior to halftime: I wasn't about to go back in the game and play again. It wouldn't have made any difference if they had threatened to shoot me. I was done.

At halftime, Doc assisted me in slowly removing my shoulder pads. Dr. Houston, Doc and I looked at my elbow, wrist, and forearm, which were now swollen three times larger than normal size. My fingers wouldn't move. For the first time since I knew Doc I heard compassion in his voice. I looked into his eyes and I saw a totally different man; I saw someone who genuinely cared. I realized there was a difference between pain and injury-I was injured, and he knew it. His treatment and compassion for a seriously injured player would be more humane than I believed he had the capacity to show.

Several times during the second half, Doc walked up to my side and asked me if I was okay. He had given me a few painkillers at halftime, and I was not in severe pain, but I was more than a little uncomfortable.

When the game ended, I would be X-rayed and scheduled for surgery. I wasn't alone, as my teammate and future roommate, Bruce Martin, an all-Conference defensive tackle, would join me in the surgical and physical rehabilitation process after he tore his anterior cruciate ligament in his knee later in the same game.

Over the next six months, I would have surgery to remove the shattered bone fragments in my right elbow and would endure the long rehabilitation process. During my weeklong stay in Lourdes Hospital in Paducah, Kentucky, the only people from Murray State University who contacted me and asked about my well-being were offensive coordinator Carl Oakley, Dr. Houston, and Doc.

In July of 1983, I was named the head football coach at Murray High School in the same community where I had played college ball. Over the next three seasons, I took several of my young high-school players to visit this gruff, hard-core, college athletic trainer. Although it was outside of his realm of responsibility, Doc saw each of my players, and with each visit I saw more human compassion and caring than I witnessed had in my college career. Doc treated these high-school athletes with a kinder and gentler touch. He was a good man and a great trainer, but he just didn't want the majority of the college athletes he treated to know that he had compassion in his heart.

It might have lessened his ability to make them ready to play in pain - without that characteristic, a college football player has no chance for success, and a trainer is soon without a career.

HOOVER TRAINER

It was the 9th of July, 2004, when I entered the home of Brandon and Marci Sheppard, two years and fifteen days since Victor's death. The couple had been married for three, and a half years and their affection for each other was evident.

I knew Brandon, but not as well as I knew the assistant coaches for the Hoover High team. He had worked under Jim Madaleno (who would later become the head trainer at the University of Kentucky during the same time I was an assistant coach for Kentucky) while attending Valdosta State University. During our summer camp in 1999, Propst asked Madaleno for a recommendation for a trainer for his Hoover football team. Madaleno recommended Sheppard for the job, and a few days later, Propst offered him the job. Sheppard accepted.

Several times over the next five years, Propst and his assistants would praise Sheppard's talents and work ethic to me. He had that unique ability to bring players back to functional playing capacity, while only missing a minimal amount of practice and game time. As Hoover's state championships began to mount, so did Sheppard's reputation for being one of the top trainers in the State of Alabama.

During my interview, Sheppard confided that prior to Victor's tragedy he had wondered how he would deal with the death of an athlete. He occasionally pondered what his response, professionally and emotionally, would be if one of his own athletes were to go down on the field in a life-threatening or dangerous situation. Would he respond in time? Would he follow the proper procedures?

He silently hoped and prayed he would never have to find out.

Marci wanted to surprise her husband for his 30th birthday by providing him the opportunity to fulfill one of his fantasies: driving a NASCAR racing vehicle at speeds up to 160 mph around the famed Talladega race track.

After taking the required prep course to drive the vehicle, an unexpected emergency arose moments before Sheppard entered the race car: An elderly man collapsed and went into cardiac arrest. Sheppard followed his training and immediately began CPR, with the help of a nurse, who was also waiting to drive. Despite their best efforts, the elderly man died.

Shaken, but not to the point of allowing the tragic event to deter him, Sheppard entered the race car with no hesitation to begin his 160-mph trip around the Talladega track. The unexpected tragedy reminded him that each moment is precious and there are no guarantees for tomorrow.

Most trainers will go their entire careers and never have a situation of life and death involving anyone, especially one of their players. Sheppard had just experienced performing CPR to the best of his ability, yet coming up short in saving another human's life. Although each life is precious, at least this time it was an elderly man and not one of his young players. The thought of losing one of his players was something he couldn't imagine.

The NASCAR experience was an exhilarating, life-changing day. He had experienced the joy of love and sharing, which his wife Marci had provided, yet in the same hour he had witnessed firsthand the tragic death of another human.

THE DEMEANOR

Similar to Doc, Sheppard had developed a style of keeping the players, and his fond feelings for them, at a distance. He was somewhat cold, hard, intense, and focused at all times. I reminded him that all trainers were cold and hard out of necessity. As he spoke to me, I could sense by his oft-blinking eyes that he had since softened his sometimes cold demeanor in his daily dealings with the players since Victor's death.

"I didn't know D that well. He was mostly a JV player during his sophomore season and had only recently been designated as a potential starter on the varsity football team," Sheppard said.

On a team with more than 200 players in grades nine through 12, it isn't uncommon for a trainer not to know each player until he has to treat them or they become a regular varsity starter.

Victor was the type of player who never entered the training room unless he was seriously injured. Sheppard knew about Victor's reputation as a tough and exciting player from listening to the other players talk about his potential, and his never-ending smile. He knew there was something special about Victor, but he just wasn't quite sure what it was.

On the day Victor died, Sheppard had tried to vacate the Hoover facility several times, only to be called back for one thing or another. This was his off-time and he was not being paid in the summer months for working with the athletes. He was talking to athletic director Ron Swann from the second-story athletic center, when, through the glass windows overlooking the practice field, they both noticed a player on his knees. At the same moment, his two-way Nextel radio buzzed, and Coach Moore told him Victor had gone down; his assistance was needed.

Immediately, he ran down the flight of steps and down the steep incline onto the practice field, where he began to assess the situation. After corresponding with Coach Watson and me, as well as analyzing and evaluating the situation, Sheppard soon commanded, "Let's start CPR. I'll do the breathing. Todd, you do the chest compressions, and I'll count for you."

Victor gasped the last of his agonal (last chance) breaths as Watson and Sheppard began the CPR. As Sheppard lowered himself to Victor and placed his lips perfectly over his, he remembered the newly acquired defibrillator, which had recently been donated by Hoover alumni Jimbo Parsons. The device could assist in the lifesaving attempt and was in storage in the training room. He silently calculated it would take at least four minutes for someone to run and grab the machine, and return with it. He could hear the ambulance siren in the background and decided the EMS and their defibrillator would arrive quicker than someone running to the training room.

Life or death decisions were made in split seconds and as Sheppard and Watson continued their CPR, Sheppard would ask himself several times, "How long will it be before the ambulance arrives?" It would only be minutes, but it seemed like hours.

In a three-day span, a 30-year-old high-school trainer would have the last breath of two humans on his lips as he blew life from his lungs into theirs, desperately trying to awaken the life in these dying men, one in his 80s and the other only 15 years of age. Sheppard remained calm, methodical, and especially professional. His face never showed worry, and his demeanor was stoic.

The EMS finally arrived and told Sheppard, "You're doing well! Keep going."

As the EMS crew pulled the lifesaving medical equipment out of the ambulance, Sheppard and Watson continued CPR until one of the EMS team told Sheppard to back away while he put the intubation device down Victor's throat. The EMS crew followed the audible commands of the defibrillator and began the process of allowing the machine to do its job.

Despite everyone's efforts, Sheppard began to believe for the second time in three days that he was going to fail in an attempt to resuscitate a dying human.

As the ambulance began to drive off the practice field, Sheppard noticed the look of desperation in the players' eyes as he peered out the ambulance windows while continuing to monitor Victor's status. He continued to work with the EMS, while praying for Victor's life every one of the next ten minutes as they maneuvered I-459 and I-65 at high speeds in the afternoon traffic of metro Birmingham.

Sheppard's experience at the NASCAR Talladega track two days before had prepared him for the high speeds, and the CPR he had performed on the elderly gentleman had given him an opportunity to psychologically prepare for human contact in a life or death situation. It did not prepare him for the discourteous rush-hour traffic, however, as numerous cars made no effort to clear a pathway for the speeding ambulance, nor did it prepare him for the psychological havoc of having one of his own players dying in front of him as several teammates watched.

When they finally arrived at the hospital, approximately ten minutes from their departure, Sheppard began to look for Victor's mother Cheryl. He wanted to spare her the sight of her son hooked up to the lifesaving machines- near death, or possibly already dead. From a distance, he spotted a frantic and grieving woman moving toward him, and although he had never met her before, he knew it was Victor's mother.

Believing it to be in the best interest of Victor and Cheryl, he stopped her and told her the best thing for her to do to help Victor was to let the EMS and doctors do their job. She honored his request.

Two years later, Sheppard struggles with whether or not he made the right decision. Not allowing, or encouraging, Cheryl to touch her son seemed to be the professional choice at the time, but he wonders if it was the humane choice, especially now, knowing it would be the last time she could have touched her son while maybe still alive. In his effort to protect Cheryl, he wonders if he robbed her of a final chance to say goodbye.

Marci called Brandon while he was in the waiting room. A few seconds later, she heard a scream through the phone, a wail unlike anything she had heard before. Victor had just been pronounced dead, and the waiting room had turned into an emotional screaming zone, with loved ones and friends making no attempt to hide their broken hearts. Brandon told Marci he loved her as he hung up the phone.

Sheppard would spend the next few months showing no emotion. He knew it was his job to comfort, to explain, and to be there for the players as they searched for reasons why this happened and wondered if it could happen to them. It would be August before Sheppard would be able to show emotion- and it was anger, not tears, that appeared first.

When Birmingham NBC newsman Jim Dunleavy made an inspirational and emotional speech at Riverchase Community Church about Victor, Sheppard noticed him becoming angry with himself. Why was everyone so capable of expressing their emotions, yet he was unable to feel anything but numbness most of the time?

Marci noticed Brandon struggling with his feelings over the next several months. He was irritable and sometimes short at home. His mind seemed to be a thousand miles away. She knew he was struggling with his need to continue his job as an athletic trainer, while dealing with his own broken heart and the unexplainable lack of emotion.

Victor had silently cried, "Fix me, Doc," and Brandon was unable to honor his dying request. He needed to cry, to scream, to shout, to do anything to let the pain release, but he couldn't. And Marci felt helpless in assisting him to find a way.

It would take another inexplicable near-tragic event, to allow Sheppard to feel again, to lose the emotional numbness that had buried itself inside him with Victor's death.

Why can't I cry? Why can't I show any emotions? Sheppard asked himself.

The answer was simple. Sheppard perceived himself as a professional. Any crack in his emotional armor might mean the end of his career as a successful athletic trainer.

Two weeks later, Sheppard was back on the job. He wanted to make sure the players were not afraid. He assured them that what happened to Victor was an unusual medical occurrence that randomly occurs to one in 100,000 people, and they had no reason to be fearful as they began their practice sessions in the sweltering July heat.

He never noticed himself changing their practice habits. Water was consistently available to the players, just as it had been before Victor's death. Injuries were immediately diagnosed and treated, just as they had been before. Players were taped and padded to protect any previous injuries, or to prevent the possibility of an injury during practice, just as they had been before.

Although Sheppard believed he changed nothing, all the players I interviewed noticed a considerable difference in Sheppard's methods, as well as the daily routines of the assistant coaches. Each player I interviewed said they were consistently told to drink more water and take more breaks. Several players said the tone of the voices of the coaches and the training staff showed more concern with their safety and health than ever before. Even though every coach and trainer had been given hard evidence that there was nothing they could have done to prevent Victor's collapse, they obviously had subconscious doubts.

Each assistant coach, as well as Sheppard, never noticed their unintentional, extra empathy and concern. Their subconscious actions were more protective than they could imagine.

Sheppard agrees that over the next two years he allowed himself to become much closer to players than he ever had before. It wasn't a conscious effort as much as it was a subconscious reality. He had missed out on knowing a very special young man because he had maintained the personality and rough exterior needed to perform his job.

Eventually, with the assistance of and continued education by Sheppard, the players overcame their subconscious fear of dying on the field during the 2002 season and won the 6A State Championship. It was an emotional season for everyone, and Sheppard was glad when it was over. Now he could relax and help with the other sports, without the fear of death in the eyes of each player he worked with. It was a strange season in the life of a trainer. Each time a player was out of breath or bent over in pain, there was a subconscious fear that showed on everyone's face, an instinctive fear of dying or seeing someone else die. It was natural, of course, but the everyday pressure was something Sheppard never wanted to deal with again.

NEVER TWICE

Thank God for basketball season! Sheppard wouldn't have to worry about potential paralyzing collisions or the heat. He could focus on the less serious injuries of basketball: ankle sprains and dislocated fingers; at least that's what he thought.

If the odds worked the way they were supposed to, Sheppard would never have to deal with a life-and-death situation for the rest of his career as an athletic trainer. Oh, sure, there may be close calls and scary situations, but never again would he have the life of another human clinging to his every decision.

Life-and-death situations are rare in high-school sports. The chance of an athletic trainer being involved once in his career is very unlikely, but to have it happen more than once, especially in the same year, would be similar to the odds of winning the lottery.

There would be an occasional false alarm from a well-meaning-coach or player, such as the day an assistant football coach witnessed a band member over heat, and called Sheppard on his two-way radio, similar to the call he received the day Victor went down, telling him to hurry onto the field and bring the defibrillator. His voice was frantic, and Sheppard sprinted onto the field.

It was a false alarm, and Sheppard was infuriated with the panic nature of the situation. Nobody is going to die! It just doesn't happen! Not again!

It was February 3, 2003, less than eight months since Victor died, when a student ran into the training room and screamed for Sheppard. Sophomore basketball player Ashley Shepherd had just finished sprinting down the court, when a strange feeling compelled her to sit down. She reached the wall at the south end of the Hoover gymnasium and slowly sat down, leaning against the wall and trying to regroup from the strange sensation in her body. That's all she remembers.

Her friends later told her that they yelled at her and told her to get up, thinking she was dogging it.

Moments later, she slumped onto the floor and lay lifeless at the end of the basketball court. She was not responding to anyone's voice.

Sheppard took off in a sprint. Head Girl's Basketball Coach Lori Elgin had already begun the emergency plan by directing each trained coach to do their rehearsed emergency duty assignments, such as calling 911 and moving the teammates farther away from Ashley, just as the football coaches had done nearly seven months before.

He arrived within seconds from his strategically located office, which was directly above the basketball court. He bent over Ashley, looking first into her eyes, then her face and finally her lips; it was as if he was seeing the face of a ghost. The lips had turned a painful bluish color, the same color that had given him nightmares each night since Victor's death when he closed his eyes and tried to sleep. It was the color of death—the look of Victor's lips when Sheppard arrived on the scene only seven months before.

Ashley was gasping for breath, the same agonal breathing he had seen before, and his brain kept telling him it was Victor again. The unthinkable had happened. A second Hoover High athlete had fallen and was fighting for life.

This can't be real. Not in the same school. Not in the same year. Not with the same trainer, Sheppard thought, as he analyzed the situation.

Sheppard sent a student to the training room with orders to bring the defibrillator. It was less than thirty seconds away, and the EMS crew would be several minutes more. Coach Moore and boys' basketball coach Lance Weems had arrived a few seconds after Sheppard and had begun to assist by removing the students and moving Ashley to a position where the defibrillator could be hooked up.

For the third time in less than eight months, Sheppard would be challenged to find a way to save another human's life. This time, however, he would have technology on his side. CPR can be a marvelous lifesaving tool, but the chances of saving a human life increase dramatically when defibrillators are used properly.

After connecting the devices to Ashley's body, the defibrillator made its robotic answer and advised a shock. Moore and Sheppard cleared their hands as the shock was administered. No response!

My God, this can't be happening again! Please tell me it's a dream! Not twice in the same year! Not twice in the same school! Please, God, don't let this happen again! Sheppard thought.

The robotic defibrillator said to administer another shock. Sheppard administered the second shock to Ashley's body. No response!

The first two shocks administered 150 volts - then 180 volts. The machine now called for 220 volts. The EMS crew had administered three shocks on Victor, with no response, before putting him in the ambulance and taking him to the hospital. Sheppard realized he was about to administer the third shock to Ashley.

"Stand back," Sheppard ordered, as 220 volts were administered to Ashley's body.

God, please, not again!

Could it be a sign of life? Ashley moaned, and her body moved ever so slightly.

"Breathe, Ashley! Breathe, Ashley!" Sheppard and Moore encouraged.

Sheppard hoped the machine would tell him the job was over, and that Ashley could now breathe on her own.

"Please, dear God, let her live! Breathe Ashley. Breathe, Ashley!"

Their prayers were answered. No shock advised! Sheppard and Moore continued to talk to Ashley, encouraging her to continue to breathe. The EMS crew arrived and said the same words they had spoken on June 24, 2002, "You're doing well. Keep going!"

The defibrillator was working on its own, continuing to help Ashley fight for her life. With the same precision as the June 24, 2002 crew, the EMS staff disconnected the Hoover defibrillator and hooked their machines to her.

Moments later, Sheppard climbed into the ambulance and began the same ride, the same pathway, the same prayers, as he had done with Victor on June 24, 2002. As they passed vehicle after vehicle, it seemed as if the same cars were on the road, still making no attempt to get out of the way as they made their way to the same Brookwood Medical Center where Victor was pronounced dead. Something was different this trip. Ashley was breathing. Ashley was alive.

The hospital personnel began asking questions. Could someone have put something in a drink? Was Ashley taking drugs? The same questions asked about Victor.

When Ashley's mother Kathy arrived at the hospital nearly one hour after Ashley's arrival, she went to Sheppard and said, "You just saved my daughter's life!"

Sheppard's thoughts went to heaven as he thanked God for allowing Ashley to live. He thought about Victor and realized it was his spirit that helped guide him through every step of the way to save this young girl's life.

And then it happened. Sheppard was able to feel emotions again, to look inside his heart and see where he had been. Victor's tragic death had prepared him to save Ashley. The answer to why Victor was so special was now firmly planted in Sheppard's mind. He knew without a doubt that if Victor had been given this choice, to give his life to better prepare Sheppard to save Ashley's, he would have willingly accepted his role. Maybe he did.

Ashley has an implanted pacemaker defibrillator today, and lives an active and productive life while attending college at the University of Alabama. She and her twin sister Amanda are actively involved in educating people throughout the United States about the life-saving abilities of defibrillators.

Victor's death helped save Ashley. Sheppard believes that God put Victor and him in Hoover High School to save Ashley and to eventually teach hundreds of others to do the same.

After the death of Victor, The Hoover City School system still only had one defibrillator at the high school. After Ashley's life was saved, the school system placed more than forty defibrillators in the Hoover schools. They are strategically located in order to be able to save the next young person's life, if the need arises.

Chapter 6

Captain Of The Ship

God, family, and football are the three things that matter most to the majority population of crazed Alabama football fanatics, and not necessarily in that order. Rush Propst, one of the most fervent and qualified teachers in Alabama football history, has diligently tutored me over the last seven years of our relationship about the passion and history of the game in this, my favorite State, which has become a second home to me.

His name always stirs emotions. It could be love or hate, sometimes both, and very little in between. I can honestly say I have loved him and hated him at the same time - and with good reason for both.

The question was: How would this man of passion, God, and football handle the tragic death of one of his all-time favorite players? Would he fail miserably in his attempt to make the team refocus on their goal of a state championship? Would he go overboard in a valiant attempt to respect Victor's memory, instead making it seem tawdry or fake? Would he alienate heavy-pocketed and much-needed boosters in his attempt to preserve the memory of Victor by taking away from the deeds of their own children?

This would indeed be a task for an unusual and strong man, a man of purpose, reserve, and conviction - but primarily a man with laser-like focus when it came to his football program. It would take the type of man who could juggle each of these duties and perform them with delicate and subtle precision. Propst would accept the challenge and attack it with the same passion and preparation as he did when preparing for his next opponent. Failure was not an option, as this challenge involved the mental welfare and future of his players the one thing that always came first with him.

I think about a ship sinking, and all the passengers and crew desperately fighting for survival, while one person stands calmly above the fray, making decisions with surgical-like precision. One thing and one thing only matters to the captain, saving the passengers lives. All else is secondary.

Propst was the captain of this ship and the players were his passengers.

It is his blessing, as well as his curse. His life had a singleness of purpose: Win football championships and make men of his players. Anything or anyone who got in his way in his attempt to accomplish this goal was expendable. Ruffling feathers and creating controversy had become a way of life. One thing not open for debate, however, and that is the indisputable fact that he continues to accomplish both of those goals.

THE BAYOU

I checked my watch every five minutes and glanced at the door to see if he was walking in. Maybe I had come to the wrong place. Even though it was my first trip to the Mobile, Alabama area, it would have been difficult to have made a mistake. The coach had given me specific instructions, and there couldn't be too many bars in this quaint bayou town.

Earlier that day I had made a recruiting visit to Alma High School, a small school south of Mobile located in the *Forrest Gump's* movie home of "Bubba," otherwise known as Bayou La Batre. I met a colorful, to say the least, high-school football coach by the name of Rush Propst. It was the spring of 1998, and I had requested to recruit the state of Alabama because I believed our (University of Kentucky) nationally televised, goal-post downing victory in the fall of 1997 over the once great national football power, University of Alabama, would open some recruiting doors for us in this football-talent rich state.

Propst was the athletic director and head football coach. One year later he would be chosen to oversee the consolidation of Alma High School with Grand Bay High School, to form Bryant High. It would be at Bryant where Propst would begin to make his name known statewide, as they immediately became a force to be reckoned with in the powerful 6A football classification.

The job was a renewal in Propst's coaching life. Although winning big at Eufaula High School, Propst had been terminated in a controversial decision by the school system that would eventually win him a settlement in a bitter lawsuit against his former employer.

After waiting an hour and drinking a couple of Bud Lights, I decided that my new coaching pal, Propst, wasn't showing up and might not be the most reliable coach I had dealt with. I paid my tab and left the establishment wondering if I would ever come back to this famous shrimpboat town.

The next day, as I made a few recruiting visits to local high schools in the Mobile area, my phone rang. Propst was on the other line. He never mentioned why, or even acknowledged that, he had never shown up the night before. Later, I would discover that his not showing up wasn't an uncommon occurrence, although not always intentional.

I silently acknowledged to myself that it didn't really matter. It is simply part of college football recruiting. You must learn to kiss high school coaches' asses because one day they may have a great player, and you can't blow an opportunity to recruit their kids. Alma linebacker/running back Brandon Johnson, who would eventually be a starter at Auburn University, was a potential impact player who wasn't heavenly recruited early in the evaluation process, and I felt we had a good chance to sign him. We talked for a few minutes and agreed to meet for lunch at Catalina's, a popular seafood establishment in Bayou La Batre.

It was in this small hometown restaurant in May of 1998 that I first witnessed the powerful seduction ability of Propst as he held court with a group of local boosters. He kept them enthralled and hanging on his every word for close to two hours as he spoke about the upcoming season, as well as his college football forecast. Propst's tendency to occasionally name-drop big-time college coaches as if they were his running buddies moved each of these boosters to the edge of their seats, clinging to his every word as if there might be a secret formula uttered with his next breath.

Propst is a master of one-on-one communication skills, and in this state where football is a close second to God, at least in the power broker vocabulary, one had better be a masterful manipulator. Raising money, especially in the economically deprived Mobile school systems, was a necessity for success, and Propst was the best at probing boosters to dig deep in their pockets to give his team an edge.

I occasionally joined the lighthearted banter with the

group of men for an hour or more when one of them playfully, but with a mild tone of sarcasm, asked me why I thought I could recruit a good Alabama high-school player to play football at the "basketball" school of Kentucky. When I responded with a vivid description of the goalpost victory over their beloved Alabama, Propst cackled loudly his approval for my spunk. With a spontaneous burst of laughter, he acknowledged that I had held my own with his feisty Alabama homeboys. We had just begun a special kinship that would take us through many journeys over the next seven years.

We talked almost daily, referring to each other at times in our lives when we needed guidance, or simply wanted a friendly ear to talk football, family, or our similar lust for exploring life's limits.

Propst would stand me up on other occasions over the next seven years, but I simply accepted it as part of his persona and never let it interfere with our friendship. I chose to believe he was similar to me in our mutual ability to move from one event to the next, sometimes with an unintended fading memory (in other words, we both suffered from the now conveniently labeled and politically correct term AADD – Adult Attention Deficit Disorder). At least we both have excuses for our failure to finish or follow up with some of our not-so-important duties or commitments.

THE MAKING OF A COACH

Most people who have known Propst closely over the years have hot and cold relationships with him. His single-minded quest for victories, as well as his passion to live life to the fullest, has made it easy to admire him while simultaneously despising him. We always look for ways to knock people down when they climb the ladder to its highest rung. They make for an easy target when they stand alone at the top.

It is impossible not to be amazed at his coaching abilities. He once taught an offensive pass play's read progression completely backwards for an entire season and still made it work for twelve victories.

His perfection, boisterous, and demanding style is effervescent and seldom hard to identify. Players respond to his presence, aura, and coaching style in win-producing ways that very few men have been able to match in the coaching profession. There is an old saying concerning legendary Alabama football coach Paul "Bear" Bryant that went something like this: "He can take his players and beat yours, and then turn around and take your players and beat his." That is the ultimate compliment in coaching and Propst would eventually be recognized as that once-in-a-lifetime type of coach.

Success didn't happen overnight for Propst. He had a productive playing career as a wide receiver/safety at Ohatchee High School, where his team lost only two regular season games, but failed to win a championship. He would continue his playing days in college, where he had a modest career as a backup wide receiver at Jacksonville State University.

The fire to win his own championship would be further fueled when his younger brother Phillip, a linebacker and tight-end, would celebrate a state championship two years after Rush's graduation. Led by legendary coach Ragan Clark, the Ohatchee championship would light a fire in his heart, probing him to think about a possible career as a coach.

Clark had been like a second father to Propst in his playing days at Ohatchee. His continued leadership and state championship season with his brother made Propst respect him even more. Clark was a hardnosed, outspoken, and sometimes intimidating coach, whom Propst would attempt to emulate throughout his career. The two men would eventually coach together at Ashville High School, after Propst began his coaching career as an assistant under Dennis MaGovirk at Cleburne High for four years, before a one-year stint under Joel Williams at Cherokee High in Canton, Georgia.

MaGovirk would teach Propst about the importance of organization, paying attention to details, and staff cohesiveness, while Williams would expand Propst's mind in the passing game. But it was Clark who gave Propst the full array of coaching experiences that would help manufacture the persona many people know today.

Clark once called Propst and another assistant, Bill Clark (Ragan's son and one of the top head coaches in Alabama today, serving as head coach of Prattville High) into his office, where he threatened to fire both of them. After a 0-10 season, he lit a fire under Propst's butt that he has never forgotten. Clark taught him that no matter what their personal relationship was, he could be fired, even though he was spared this time. Propst has used the same motivational ploy with some of his own staff over the years.

After helping lead Ashville to their first 3A playoff appearance in school history, as well as experiencing a 0-10 season, Propst was working hard to consistently improve as an assistant coach but still unsure if he was head coaching material. His ascent to his first head coaching job came unexpectedly when he was asked—and accepted to take over the head coaching job from Clark in the summer of 1989, after Clark resigned following the tragic death of his wife Judy in an auto accident.

Propst would compile a respectable 26-20 record for the

next four seasons, including a horrendous 1-9 season in 1990 and a banner best-ever 12-2 year and trip to the semi-final round of the playoffs in 1992. The news media caught a glimpse of this young, brash head coach who had taken an historically downtrodden program to a near championship season. Propst's honeymoon with the news media had begun, and because of his exceptional personal relationship skills (in other words, he knows whose butt to kiss and when) continues to this day!

The next stop for Propst was at the larger classification, 5A: Eufaula High, where Propst went 25-20 in his second head coaching stint. This much higher profile job would provide a rollercoaster of emotions.

His wife Tammy was leaving the 1994 spring game with their two young sons, Bryan and Jacob, who were only 13 months and 30 months old, when she had a horrible car crash. Miraculously, neither boy was seriously hurt, but Tammy would suffer life-threatening injuries that would require her to spend three months in the hospital, as well as continue treatment and rehab for years to come. To make matters worse, on September 21, 1994, in the middle of a 3-7 season, Propst would lose his father Clifford to stomach cancer.

Eufaula fans and administration would be patient with Propst through his tragedy-laden 1994 season, but after a 5-5 record in the 1995 season, Propst was convinced he would soon be fired. The Eufaula faithful decided to give him one more chance, and Propst made the best of it with an 11-2 record.

Most coaches with 11-2 records are rewarded with raises and pats on the back, but Propst had made some enemies who were hell-bent on getting rid of him at any cost, and he would eventually be fired after the spectacular season. Refusing to accept his fate, he filed suit against the school district and began a legal battle that would not end until he reached an out-of-court settlement in 1999, his first year as head coach of Hoover.

Rumors swirl whenever a coach is fired, but if you are fired after an 11-2 season, and a lawsuit is filed, not only will you be the talk of the local coffee shops and talk radio throughout the State, you will also become the subject of discussion amongst the statewide network of school administrators who must make decisions about whom to hire.

"Should we consider hiring a controversial coach with rumors swirling about his firing and a lawsuit pending, or should we simply move on to the next candidate," is a question that is almost universally answered 'No!" as administrators will almost always hire the less controversial candidate.

With no success in finding another job, Propst had to move on and eventually decided to take his insurance license exam and explore the world of sales as a possible new profession. He had begun to enjoy his quiet life of fishing, golfing, and hunting, as well as spending quality time with his family, and had even contemplated what a life without football might be like. It was going to take a special school administrator with nerves of steel to hire Propst. He thought he was dead as a coach, and he knew he needed a guardian angel to step up and help him.

Terry Curtis and Robert Higginbotham, head coaches of Murphy High and Shades Valley at the time, were two of the most successful and respected coaches in the state of Alabama. When they were chosen to coach in the prestigious Alabama-Mississippi All-Star game in the summer of 1997—Higginbotham as head coach and Curtis as his offensive coordinator—they called Propst to see if he would come join them as their defensive coordinator. Propst accepted and relished the opportunity to get back on the football field, albeit only for one week.

When Propst looked at the lineup of offensive players for the Mississippi All-Star Team, he knew why he had been named the defensive coordinator. No coach in their right mind would want to try and stop this lineup for Mississippi, which included future NFL star running backs Deuce McCallister and Johnny Avery, as well as future University of Mississippi All-SEC quarterback Romaro Miller, and several future NFL linemen. This was a challenge unlike any other Propst had tackled in his coaching career, and he relished the opportunity.

One thing was certain: If he could find a way to stop this superb group of Mississippi All-Stars, his reputation in the coaching profession would skyrocket overnight.

When the Alabama team won the game in a 10-6 defensive struggle, Propst was lauded publicly, and even more importantly, in private, by Curtis and Higginbotham to their numerous contacts of high-school administrators. Propst's love affair with the media grew as he was given numerous accolades for his defense's performance.

More important was the fact that Alba High School principal Ed Latham, unbeknownst to Propst, had watched some of the practices and the game. Latham was impressed and decided to take a chance on this controversial coach, offering him the job as the athletic director at Alma High School, with a conditional promise to make Propst the head football coach the following year when Alma would consolidate with Grand Bay to form Bryant High School.

Propst was ecstatic and eventually accepted the job, but only after being rejected for one of the dream jobs of his life. He had interviewed for the head coaching job of his hometown high school and alma mater, Ohatchee High (most of us coaches have this same fantasy about going home and winning a championship in front of our hometown friends—including this writer who was also rejected for a coaching job in his home town) and had become infatuated with the thoughts of returning home to lead Ohatchee to a State title. It wasn't meant to be, as he received that dreaded "thanks, but no thanks" phone call when he was told the school system had decided to go in another direction.

Without the trust of Curtis and Higginbotham, Propst would probably be sitting on a couch today, somewhere in the state of Alabama, convincing some unsuspecting soul to buy one million dollars more of life insurance than they thought they needed. Many poor widows could have benefited if Curtis and Higginbotham had never made that call to Propst.

Grateful would be an understatement when describing Propst's feelings for Curtis (who is the head coach of UMS-Wright in Mobile today) and Higginbotham (now the head coach of Tuscaloosa County). When Higginbotham called me and asked to become a client of mine prior to the 2003 season, I made a call to Propst to inform him and ask for his approval. Because of his incredible success, and his assistance in generating new clients for me, I had given Propst the power to blackball any school in Alabama from becoming a client of mine. Although I knew the story of how Higginbotham had helped Propst's career, he was also a potential foe whom Propst might have to face in the playoffs year after year.

"Hell, yes, he can become your client! If not for Robert Higginbotham, I wouldn't be a coach today. I'd rather he win the State championship than me!" Propst shouted through the phone.

I never knew what to expect from Propst, as his decisions ranged from one extreme to the other, but in this case there was no doubt he remembered who had helped him when he was down.

MOVING UP

When Propst accepted the Hoover job in April of 1999, he took over a struggling program. Gerald Gann, who had previously been successful as a head coach for Homewood High before taking the Hoover job, and continues his success for his current employer John Carroll High, had experienced an 11-2 season in 1995 before falling to records of 3-7, 3-7, and 4-6 the three previous years before Propst's arrival. There was a rich tradition from many years past (under the old school name of Berry High), with appearances in State championship games in 1969, 1977 (won), 1982(tied), and 1988 under the helm of the legendary coach Bob Finley.

Tragedy had taken Finley away from the Hoover faithful when he suffered a fatal heart attack while mowing one of the Berry practice fields, days before coaching his first summer practice for the newly built and named Hoover High.

By the time Propst took the job, the Hoover fans and boosters were starving for a return to the glory days of Berry and Finley. They certainly weren't afraid of hiring a controversial coach, who was still involved in a lawsuit with a former employer, especially since Propst had just been named Alabama Coach of the Year.

After his first and only year at the newly consolidated Bryant High ended with an 11-1 record, he went from being an enigma only a few years before to becoming a hot coaching commodity. The fast growing, affluent suburb outside of Birmingham would aggressively pursue their man and pull him away from the school and principal who had revived his almost dead career.

His impact at Hoover was immediate, as they opened with a 7-3 record in his first season in 1999. The 2000 season would begin his Hall of Fame type run of 70-4 over the next five years with the Buccaneers winning four of five 6A State championships. His 2004 team finished with his first undefeated season (15-0) and was ranked as high as No. 4 in the nation by the *USA Today* high school poll.

It only seems natural that Propst would join the ranks of the college coaching profession. He is a youthful 46 years of age with a good twenty-plus years of coaching ahead. There is no one coach I have known over the years who would make a better college coach. He has all the necessary ingredients: great coach on the field, players play hard for him out of fear and respect, he can sell snow to Eskimos - in other words he can recruit any southern Joe Bob to come play football for any local college in America. And he has that final ingredient necessary to make any man a great college coach: He will cut his best friend's heart out if it will help him win the next championship.

A calculated ruthlessness of staying single-minded is a necessity to being a championship college coach today. The rare ability to focus on one single mission - winning games - takes an unusual individual with numerous positive leadership characteristics, along with some characteristics that border on ruthless. Propst has all of them, the good and the controversial.

So why then would this top-notch coach not have offers to coach in college football? The answer is very simple. Many college head coaches might question whether he can follow, rather than being the leader. Others may have been turned off by his occasional blunt and open criticism of college coaches in general. He has, at times—both privately and publicly—attacked their ineptitude, as well as blasting an entire coaching staff when their perceived incompetence in judging talent left one of his senior players without a scholarship offer.

I have told Propst several times that his only hope of attaining a Division I college coaching job was for some idiot college athletic director (yes, there are a few) to screw up and hire me as their head coach. I'm afraid he is out of luck with that possibility!

The bottom line is that he is too good of a coach for most college head coaches to take a chance on hiring. Yes, you heard me correctly. Sometimes you can be too good at this profession. There has never been another career with bigger egos than that of Division I college head football coaches. It would take an unusual head coach who is willing to share the spotlight with a strong-willed assistant to step up and hire Propst. He might just help lead them to the promised land of a championship season. But some of those guys would rather lose than give up some of their glory.

MOMMA – THE FAN

After losing his father Clifford to colon cancer on September 21, 1994, Propst was still blessed with the guidance and support of his biggest fan, his mother Edna. She only missed two games in his entire career and one of those was to travel and see Rush's younger brother Phillip play a college game at Henderson State University in Arkadelphia, Arkansas. Even when her fight with ovarian cancer at age 73 became such a problem that she was unable to leave her bed for other simple functions of life, she would muster the strength to attend his games. On June 20, 2003, Edna died, and Propst lost his staunchest advisor and supporter.

A mutual friend called and informed me as soon as Edna died. I was coaching the Lexington Horsemen indoor football team at the time, and we were scheduled to play our first round playoff game the night before Edna was to be buried. I decided to make the seventeen-hour one-way drive from Wheeling, West Virginia to the funeral home in Anniston, Alabama immediately following the game. If I drove straight through, I knew I could be there a couple of hours before the funeral began.

Seventeen hours after the trip began, and with the assistance of several wake-up calls to my cell phone from a dear friend of mine who played alarm clock for me, I was in Anniston. Using the home of one of Propst's friends to shower and prepare for the trip to the funeral home, I frantically tried to revive myself. When I first saw Propst, I was overcome with emotion. He and Edna were very close and I knew how distraught he was. I told him I loved him and was sorry for his loss. He was very composed and thanked me for coming.

Over the five years we had known each other, he had become like family to me and I would never have forgiven myself if I hadn't made the trip, even though I guessed he probably would not have made the same trip for me under similar circumstances. That part of our relationship had been established in years long since gone. It is kind of like a marriage, where one person normally gives more than the other one to make it work. Most close relationships work that way, if they are going to survive.

The reason I tell you this is because you must understand his priorities in life to understand how he handled the tragedy of Victor's death when dealing with the players, parents, and Victor's family. He always has the ability to focus on the most important thing in his life: winning the next championship and taking care of his players. Everything else comes secondary. You either accept that, or choose to hate him for it. I chose to accept it, while still allowing myself to hate him, if only part of the time.

Propst gave a poignant and emotional eulogy for his mother, with only a few eyes remaining dry. At one point, he gave a passionate plea to the heavy-hearted group of mourners about getting right with Jesus Christ and accepting him as their Lord and Savior. I swear, I thought he glanced through the crowd, specifically searching for a chance to look me in the eye. He found me safely hidden in a back row in the far right corner and continued looking directly at me when he gave his come to Jesus talk. We had discussed our faith at times and he knew I was struggling with questions about God, but to have this tough renegade of a man with whom I had closed many night spots together over the years begin a saving-my-soul sermon, brought a huge grin to my face. This was Propst at his best - never failing to seize an opportunity in public to make a sales pitch, this time for my soul in the middle of his mother's eulogy! It was all I could do to keep from bursting out with laughter. He truly was the master salesman.

THE 2002 SEASON OF REMEMBERING

Each Hoover player on opening night of 2002 was a little more nervous than usual. There was a special buzz in the air, and as each player pulled his jersey on over his pads, he oozed with that tingle of fear and excitement that only those who have played the game can adequately explain. All the Buccaneers had a special #8 sewn into the upper left corner of their jerseys in memory of Victor.

Chad Jackson, the All American receiver and self-proclaimed cousin of Victor, was wearing #8 instead of his customary #1—the deal he had worked out with Propst to honor Victor in the first and last games of the season.

"JayRay," as 2002 Hoover running back and defensive back Justin Ray was called by his teammates and coaches, was out for the coin toss with Cheryl, Syreeta, and Cortez. As the announcer made a request for silence, the entire crowd of more than 9,000 paid their respects to Victor in prayer. A sign read: VICTOR "D" HILL - FOREVER A BUC.

Youth minister and team chaplain Terry Slay spoke into the loud speaker with a calm yet persuasive voice and reminded the players and crowd what some already knew. "Victor Hill understood his purpose in life and used his bountiful gifts to obtain that purpose daily. He was passionate, determined, and a great friend to many, some of whom he still influences today. He did the right thing, whether surrounded by people or by himself. Victor left a legacy of love, and his memory will always be with us."

When Slay finished, there were few dry eyes in the crowd or on the field.

How would the players respond to the emotions of the night? Fear, apprehension, and sadness, as well as excitement and anger swelled into the players' minds as they finished their final pre-game warm-ups before heading to the locker room.

When the Buccaneers returned to the locker room, Propst gave them his pre-game speech. It wasn't a hellfire *Win one for the Gipper* presentation. He simply reminded the players that they should always play the game as if the next play might be their last. Nothing in life is guaranteed, and their minute-to-minute passion is crucial for the chance at success.

Finally, Propst looked each player in the eye and reminded them, "Victor Hill loved this game. He *literally* gave his life to football! He will be up there watching you tonight and wishing he was here."

Robert E. Lee High School, from Montgomery, had no chance that night as the Bucs, though somewhat sloppy and not as physically aggressive as usual, would still coast to a 42-20 win.

When the game was over and the moms and dads hugged their sons and congratulated them, Cheryl returned home with tears in her eyes and a broken heart pounding with pride and sorrow as she cried herself to sleep. She was proud of Victor, but also proud of Propst for making sure her son was eloquently remembered and honored.

Propst gathered his team in the locker room, where Jackson stood with Victor's #8 jersey in his arms. The 6'1", 205-pound, perfectly sculpted Jackson showed no emotion as Propst told him to hang the jersey in Victor's locker, which had remained fully equipped and unscathed since his death. In a moment of silence, as players bowed their heads, Jackson gracefully walked over to Victor's locker and hung the jersey where it would remain for the remainder of the next three seasons, the one exception being when Jackson wore it in the State championship game in December of 2002.

Victor's locker would remain exactly as it was that night. His jersey, shoes, and all the other equipment would rest in the same place where Victor had left them on June 24th. No one would be allowed to wear the #8 jersey or use Victor's locker until Cortez became a varsity player in July of 2005.

Each day, as Hoover varsity players walk into the locker room, they continue to feel Victor's spirit. Propst made sure of it.

A PLAYER'S COACH

Many people would be surprised to know that characteristic

makes Propst the most successful, yet it is simple to identify and define. It's the one thing that many people, including his closest of friends, might not see. He deeply cares about his players and they know it. He can verbally assault and challenge them in one moment, then minutes later, hug their neck and have them smiling broadly as if the challenge never took place. He can bring them into his office and demote them from a starting position, yet have them clamoring at his office door three years after graduating, much like a dog begging for a pat on the head, just to seek his master's approval. I have known hundreds of coaches over my life, and I have seen very few show the power over a lifetime that Propst seems to have over his players. Most every decision concerning his student athletes, right or wrong, has been made because it is what he believes to be in their best interest and they eventually know it. Not only do they respect and fear him, they also love him. When you can build that type of relationship with your players, you have few limits on what you can achieve.

JayRay began the imitation of Propst with better acting skills than Denzel Washington ever dreamed of. It was perfect. The mannerisms were exquisite in detail, and the voice was so concisely similar to Propst that it could have been an earlier tape recording that had captured his every word.

The 2002 Hoover Buccaneers captured the State championship with a 14-1 season, and it was time to celebrate with the January football banquet. There wasn't a better way to start the ceremony than to bring down the house with laughter. This had been a long emotionally draining season, and humor was the best medicine to attempt to make the pain of Victor's tragedy fade, finally allowing everyone to enjoy the fruits of victory.

At the expense of the head coach, the entire group of Hoover players, coaches, parents, and boosters burst their insides with laughter. JayRay went from comparing Propst to Propst's make-believe cousin. Similar in coaching ability and mannerisms, former Florida and current South Carolina head coach Steve Spurrier and Propst were familiar with each other on and off the field. Their on-field characteristics of visor tossing and facial contortions brought the art of body language to a new level. Their egos were equally as big as their championships, and JayRay was masterfully displaying their comparisons.

Answering the never ending ring of his cell phone, while still coaching his coaches and players, is an art few can handle, but JayRay was giving the audience a colorful play-by-play example of how the AADD Coach Propst accomplished the feat. When he finally finished his Academy Award-like performance, the crowd was whipped into a frenzy of laughter, all at the expense of Propst.

I have known coaches who would have been furious and embarrassed at this good-natured but surprised ribbing. Propst, however, laughed as hard as anyone. He dropped his fierce pride and opened his soul for two reasons: 1) This was an act of love from his players, and even though the laughter came at his expense, Propst knew his players desperately needed to laugh; and (2) The heartbreak from losing one of their comrades deserved to be soothed and, as always, he would attempt to soothe it.

The banquet continued with the normal agenda of a customary banquet. Awards were given and speeches were made. Victor's presence was felt, and he was probably floating above the crowd, laughing as hard as anyone, no doubt wishing he had been able to partake with JayRay in the roasting of Propst.

All the players, parents, coaches, and administrators felt

his presence. It was impossible not to, as Propst had made sure from the day Victor was buried that he would remain a daily part of this team. The 2002 State champion Hoover Buccaneers were a team, and Victor was an integral part of the championship season. Propst made sure he was included every step of the way. When player rings and awards were announced, Victor was announced as well. Cheryl, Syreeta, and Cortez were there each step of the way to make sure Victor was receiving his part of the championship.

The pre-season motto of a championship framed poster said "RECLAIM IT," and the idea to accomplish the goal never left the mind of Propst throughout the season. When the close-up photo of the poster was examined, it mysteriously showed #8 in the bottom left corner. Victor was indeed everywhere and it would become a tribute to Propst's unique relationship and communication skills as to how he kept it from becoming a distraction.

THE MAN

In quiet times, the man who remains a mystery to many will sit in his black leather chair, staring aimlessly out the office window, and reflect on the most special player he ever coached. People look at Propst's toughness and sometimes-perceived ruthlessness, and wonder if he is even human. But it is in his moments of solace that he thinks about Victor and the countless days he would come in to visit by himself, just to relax for a moment and make Propst laugh or contemplate life. He was unlike any player Propst had coached before or since, and he could reach Propst's tender side like no other player ever had. Victor promised Propst his class was never going to lose a State championship while he played, and he said it with such conviction that Propst believed him.

A year to the day after Victor died, Propst was told someone was on the practice field sobbing. It was getting close to dark, and he instantly knew it was Cheryl. He bolted from his chair and raced to join her, hoping to console her and bring back the good memories of her son. She was in the exact spot where Victor had collapsed, crying uncontrollably. Moments after he grabbed her and held her close, his presence would begin to soothe her as they began to reminisce.

Cheryl would leave and go home to her house.

Propst would quietly walk back to his empty locker room, his second home. It, like Cheryl's home, had also never been the same since Victor's death

A few weeks later, on a Sunday afternoon in late July, 2003, only a few days before summer practice would officially start, Propst found himself wandering into the locker room. He was alone and had felt the urge to soak in Victor's spirit. Quietly, and with no one near, he sauntered up to Victor's locker and sat down in front of it, gazing ahead - at nothing in particular.

A tear slowly worked its way down his cheek as he felt the guilt again: the guilt of not being there when Victor went down. He was the head coach, and it was his job to protect his players. Although his brain keeps telling him he couldn't have done anything to save him, his heart tells him he could, and should have!

The desperate images won't leave his conscience. Each player sheepishly staring at him as he briskly walks onto the field while Victor is being driven off by the EMS. He believes they're all thinking the same thought: *The head coach is here now. He'll save him.*

They believed in Propst, and he knows it. He feels as if he let them down. The guilt won't leave him. He can handle envy, even hatred, by his coaching peers and fans, but the thought of letting his players down is nearly unbearable.

Cheryl told me no one would ever understand how much Victor loved Propst, and she never understood why until he died. It took time for her to realize that this rough-around-the-edges, old-school, fiery football coach genuinely loved her son.

It had to happen sooner or later. Better sooner than having never shown up. Most of the well-meaning parents, coaches, and players had stopped coming to see Cheryl a few weeks after Victor's death. They had their own problems and their own lives to deal with. It is understandable and normal.

I had pleaded with the coaches, players, and friends of the family at a team meeting the Wednesday after Victor's death to continue to visit the family for years to come. When tragedy strikes, families need you as the months and years go by. Not just the normal "make yourself do your duty" visit, but they also need to continually remember, to explore the past, to see his friends and hear their stories. Much of the deceased one's life was lived outside their walls, and a reflective visit from a friend can add a lifetime of new memories in their never ending broken hearts.

Still fresh in my memory was the death of my football teammate and best friend, Ernie, who died in a tragic car wreck twenty-seven years earlier in my senior year of high school. For the next twenty years, I stopped to visit his mom and dad, and especially his sister Jennie. Only in the last few years, and with immense guilt, had I not been to see her. I even missed her mom's and dad's funerals. I still remember how much their faces would glow every time I came to visit, as we would reminisce and tell the same stories over and over again, with an occasional new twist that would mesmerize us all for one fluttering moment.

One person listened intently as I gave my plea.

For the next two years, while Victor's teammates played on, and the well-intentioned visits from friends and parents of players stopped, Propst would come see her, Cortez, and Syreeta. He would stop by unexpectedly, even if it was only to chat for a moment, or hug her, or to get an update on how Cortez was dealing with life. He genuinely cared and she knew it. She also knew he was misunderstood by some boosters and parents to the point of hatred. If only they could see him now. He didn't have to be there, but he was.

Propst is a lot of things to a lot of people: passion, adventure, love, hate and fury. He is, most of all, completely loyal to his players - some might argue to a fault. His name has become somewhat legendary over the last five years, and just the mention of it can stir a stimulating and spicy conversation in any venue in the State. But one thing is certain: His love for Victor and his players is unquestionable.

He wouldn't allow Hoover to forget Victor, even after the 2002 State championship, when some people probably wanted the ceremonies for Victor to end. But Propst knew the 2003 season was even more important than the 2002 season. It was Victor's senior year, and every step along the way he remembered and included Victor with the rest of his teammates. Cheryl will never forget what he did to include her son.

Many mothers wouldn't allow their children to continue in football after having one son die on the field. In July, 2005, Cortez would take over his brother's locker and his retired #8 jersey. Cheryl believed in Propst, and she knew that he loved her son. Now she has given him a second son to learn his life lessons of toughness, teamwork and hard work.

As the head coach of any program, whether it be high school

or college, your first responsibility should always be to do your job in the method that serves the best interest of your players and your school. If that means you must personally sacrifice relationships with outsiders, or even friends, then so be it.

Propst is in a class by himself when it comes to serving his employer and doing his job. He is simply the best football coach in the state of Alabama, including the colleges. Along the way, his sometimes overzealous commitment to his players and his profession has cost him friendships, as well as bringing on the ire and spite of many opponents, and even some loyal Hoover supporters.

I am acutely aware of my strengths and my weaknesses, and while I know I am a good football coach, I also know I could not have delivered State championship seasons in the middle of a tragedy such as this one. It took a uniquely qualified individual to juggle the human elements necessary to lead a group of teenagers through the emotional rollercoaster of the 2002 and 2003 seasons. Maybe 1/10th of 1% of all the coaches in this business could have succeeded in victories, discipline, life lessons, toughness, and human compassion during such a tumultuous period.

I know only one, and his name is Propst.

You could debate whether he is moral when making some of his decisions to better his program, but what none of us can debate is the results: He wins championships, and he makes his players better prepared for life.

Cheryl now knows why she grew to love this mysterious enigma of a man.

He truly is the captain of the ship.

Chapter 7

Big Boys Do Cry

Football is about as macho a sport ever invented. We are taught from the earliest age that to be successful in the game, you must never show fear, pain, weakness, or a lack of toughness. Coaches must keep a tight upper lip in times of adversity, or else the players won't remain as tough as they have to be. Very simply put, "Big Boys Don't Cry," or do they?

MACHO MEN

"I was shopping at TJ Maxx when I got this uneasy, eerie feeling in my stomach. It's hard to explain, but something inside of me told me to go home. I was driving down the road, when my cell rang. Normally, I have the music so loud that I can't hear my cell in the car, but I barely heard the ring and answered. It was my friend Jennifer Falls," former Hoover cheerleader and close friend of Victor's since the sixth grade, Brittany Brown, recalled.

There was panic and pandemonium in Jennifer's voice, and I couldn't understand her as I asked her to slow down and tell me what was wrong. She shouted that D collapsed on the field. 'He's gone. He's gone.'

"I was driving on a narrow two-lane road and momentarily lost my composure, causing me to run my car off the road into a ditch. I was bawling, and all I could do was call my mom. I didn't need to drive anywhere, and it took my mother's strong guidance to help get me home safely.

"When I walked into Hunter Street Baptist Church a few days later, I looked at D's cold lifeless face and thought I was going to panic. I gasped for air through a river of tears, as they ran down my face.

"His mother was so strong, standing by his casket, talking to every person who came by. She couldn't have known half the people, but she would put on a smile and listen to their stories about her son. I didn't know what to say. I just wanted her to know how much I loved her son, and the words came clumsily out of my mouth as I uttered something about how everything would be okay. When I look back, I can't believe I said it, but Ms. Hill smiled and hugged me.

"The one thing that really touched me was watching the football coaches. I was so used to observing these macho men run around in their coaching shorts and whistles yelling at the players. People didn't think they had hearts or feelings.

"In a poignant and emotional moment that is permanently etched in my mind, Coach Propst stood up and addressed the crowd of more than a thousand mourners. I saw something I never thought I'd see when this tough, hard man squalled like a baby, while telling his players how much he loved them, as well as D."

"I didn't think anyone could be hurting as bad as I was until I witnessed Coach Propst's heart breaking. My mom kept rubbing my back trying to soothe me. My life was forever changed by the entire experience," Brown concluded.

SUBTLE CHANGES

They didn't notice the subtle changes, but all the players did. Each day on the field was different than it had been in the past. Offering more water breaks and spending more time with a player who thought he might be injured. They still screamed, but not with the reckless abandonment of before. The coaches who were on the field that tragic day were changed forever.

Matt Moore fits the stereotypical look of an offensive line coach. A former offensive linemen for Valdosta State University, Moore, still in his early 30s, looks as though he can bench-press a building, and could probably line up and play tomorrow if he had to. His linemen are always some of the best-coached units in the country, and his success at Hoover recently landed him the head coaching job at North Gwinnet High in Georgia in February of 2005.

Married to his college sweetheart, Kelly, they are the proud parents of two small children, Reece, 1, and Tanner, 3. If anyone besides his players recognized a change in his daily mannerisms, it would be Kelly.

"Matt went through so much in a short period of time with Victor's death and then Ashley's rescue. He probably never realized how much it changed him, but I did. He was totally different with the kids. He began to notice everything," Kelly told me late one night in the summer of 2004.

"The day after Ashley went down, Reece was experiencing some heavy breathing. Matt immediately picks her up and rushes her to the hospital. I'm not certain he would have done that before Victor and Ashley. He certainly spends more quality time with the kids than before," she added.

"I know I'm supposed to be this tough, strong-guy, offensive line coach, but the moment I walked into Hunter's Street Baptist

Church, I saw Adam Truitt (offensive linemen), and I just lost it," Matt piped in.

"You try to uphold this tough-guy image, but it was impossible. All of us who were on the field that day eventually went together to get counseling from a professional. You looked around the room, and we were all squalling like babies; so much for a bunch of tough guys," Matt quipped.

STRESS KILLS

Craig Moss and Todd Watson had both coached at Bryant High with Propst before coming to join him at Hoover. Both were Bayou men: the toughest of the tough. Born and raised with the attitude of concealing your fears, emotions, and anxiety, both men would eventually experience dramatic days of personal fear as a result of their experience on the field that June day of 2002.

"Every time a kid breathes hard, I look at him differently than before. When I first called Rush, moments after D went down on the field, I told him I thought D was dead. When the ambulance pulled off the field, I stood exactly in the spot where he had been lying for several moments. I was in shock," Moss told me, two years after Victor had passed.

"Craig expresses his feelings to me more now than ever before," his wife of more than ten years, Jennifer, said.

"And he is definitely more involved with the boys (Braylon, 6 and Brody, 2)."

"Immediately following D's death, he began to experience anxiety, depression, and eventually high blood pressure. Following the 7-on-7 tournament in July, he had chest pains that alarmed us to the point of taking him to the hospital," she stated.

"It was eerie," Craig joined in.

"Here I was in Brookwood, the same hospital D died in, thinking I'm having a heart attack in my early 30s. The results of a blood enzyme test were inconclusive, and the doctors decide to do a heart catheter."

"Thank God, he was fine. It was simply stress and reflux," Jennifer added.

"I was coaching in a daze until the Tuscaloosa County loss. Rush forced me out of it, and I went back to my old ways of coaching with more intensity," Craig concluded.

"Still, I'll never be the same. You don't forget what happened no matter how hard you try."

Watson can still recall each request he gave Victor, "Slow down, D. Breathe. Slow down. Breathe."

"I never panicked. When he first went down, he rolled over, and when I asked him to slow his breathing down, he did."

"After Brandon and I started C.P.R., I kept thinking to myself, Don't press too hard, or you'll break his sternum or ribs. Everyday the picture keeps coming back in my brain. I can't get it to go away." Watson trembled as big tears rolled down his face while he recalled that day's events.

"He called and told me to come pick him up and take him to Brookwood," his wife since 1993, Christie, added.

"Yeah, I had to keep telling her to slow down on the way there. I was afraid she was going to kill us because she was driving so fast," Todd laughed.

"He's always been good with the girls (Leigh Ashton, 9, and Micah, 1), but no doubt he is much better since Victor's tragedy," she said.

"Nobody knows what he has been through. He completely quit sleeping for a while, until the stress almost killed him. One day his heart began to throb, and the pain was severe enough that we feared the worse. I took him to the doctor. Thank God, it was just stress.

"I didn't coach the same until after the loss to Tuscaloosa County. I was embarrassed by how non-physical we were. That woke me up, and I returned to my old self. But I know I'll never be the same. I wouldn't be human if I could go through this experience and not be more empathetic to the players," Watson concluded.

OVERCOMING FEAR

Starting guard Cliff Groce reminisced about the Wednesday afternoon meeting two days after Victor's death, "We all came together as a team and talked about how we felt and where we were going to go from here. Several people stood up and spoke their mind. But the one thing that stood out to me was watching my coaches openly weep as they reminded us about how much they loved D, and us. I have never felt, as close to a group of people in my life as I did that day.

"Each of us had our own way of dealing with it. I tried to distract myself, but every time the thought of D came up, it would inspire me to play harder or get through a tough practice. I'll never forget senior night, when Ms. Cheryl came onto the field and the entire group of seniors rose to honor her and D. That team didn't have a chance that night as we annihilated them.

"The coaches were different, but they kept us focused," Groce remarked.

Linebacker Matt Joiner said he noticed the coaches coaching differently, not as tough as normal. The first scrimmage of the season, he noticed he was playing too tentatively, not with the required reckless abandonment he had to have to be successful.

However, after the opening night pre-game ceremonies to remember Victor, it all came back. "I realized how lucky I was to be alive and able to play football. Nobody loved the game as much as D. We all looked up to him and the celebration of his life before the game took away any apprehension or fear I may have had."

"I was afraid when we went to camp at Jacksonville State, only a few weeks after D's death. The heat was unbelievable, and on more than one occasion, I gasped for breath and wondered if it was going to be my last one," recalled former teammate and friend Drew Hall.

"People sometimes have the misconception that we won the state championship for D. That's not true. We won it for our team, and D never left our team. He was always a part of us. He wouldn't have wanted us to win just for him because he knew it was a team game more than anyone.

"Every close game someone would yell, 'What would D do,' and we would become re-energized and find a way to win. That's how we kept him on the field with us. We still used his energy, just like we would have if he were on the field screaming at us.

"Coach, the hard thing for me is to walk into my dad's office (Randy Hall and Cheryl have worked together for a few years) and see Ms. Cheryl. I don't know what to say, so I avoid seeing her at times. It feels weird. I know that as much as it hurts me to have D gone, it has to be unbearable to her," Hall stated.

Deontai Clemmons remembered how unmanly he felt when he was bawling like a baby, until he looked around the room and saw his entire offensive line teammates joining him. "All that manliness went out the window.

"We were winning, but something was definitely missing.

We weren't as tough and physical as we needed to be. After the Tuscaloosa County loss, Coach Propst had a brutal drill called 'Spike Drill,' where our manhood was challenged in front of all our teammates. It was what we needed, and it definitely brought us out of our funk."

DRY EYES

I only saw two dry eyes in the crowd of more than 100 football players and coaches gathered in the Hoover High School theatre, and they belonged to 6' 1," 245-pound middle linebacker Curtis Dawson.

"I'm not the emotional type. We all loved Victor and we must remember what he would have wanted us to do: Win and keep playing hard," Dawson said.

Two years later, we met at the Barnes & Noble bookstore in the Summit Shopping Center in Mountain Brook.

"Coach, I never cry. It's just not me. Sometimes I wish I could, but I can't. People don't understand, and they think I don't care, but I loved D as much as anyone. Nobody knows the number of times we would run the hills together getting ready for football season. We only lived two minutes from each other, and his mom and mine (Cassandra Dawson) were best friends.

"The day he died, we were walking down the hill toward the practice field, and I was complaining to D that I didn't want to go through another practice session, when he looked me in the eye and said I couldn't be tired, and I had better get crunked up and then jogged onto the field. He never got tired.

"I never thought he was going to die. This was Hoover High. We had the best of everything. None of us could die out there - but he did!

"Cheryl came to me after he was dead in a daze. She grabbed me and shook me, telling me to go wake D up. 'Curtis, he'll listen to you. No one else can do it! Go wake him up.'

"Every week, we would be taking the field or walking into the huddle, when Brandon Brown (teammate) would start yelling, 'What would D do?' You couldn't help but remember him every game because Brandon or someone else would yell out his name.

"Honestly, though, I never used it for motivation until it happened one game without me even thinking about it. We were playing Vestavia in the State semi-finals, and it was the last play of the game. They were on the one yard line, and this was the play to win or lose the game. If they score, they go to Legion Field for the State championship game. If we stop them, we go.

"I was totally exhausted and didn't have enough left in me to make a play, and it was pretty obvious that they would run the quarterback sneak right at me. For the first time since D died, he came to me on the field. I remembered him running down the hill before practice right before he died, telling me I couldn't be tired and to get crunked up.

"When the ball was snapped, I had no doubt I would make the play. With defensive linemen Steven Tajer and Matt Jackson exploding under Vestavia's offensive line, we were able to help stop their quarterback inches from the goal line. I knew D was with me and I grinned as I thought about him when I was getting up from the pile, knowing we were going to Legion Field.

"I don't know if it's good or bad, but I still haven't cried. It's just not what I do," Dawson said, as he shook my hand and walked away.

Big boys do cry, just not all of them.

Chapter 8

Why, God?

Defensive lineman and classmate Jeff Haag had just hung up the phone, and Deontai Clemmons was fumbling for words and thoughts. Haag heard a television report that a Hoover football player had died on the field, and he was calling Clemmons to see if he knew what was going on. All Clemmons could do was murmur to himself, "Please don't let it be D, God. Please don't let it be D!"

"It was as if I already knew the answer and was only preparing myself for the inevitable," Clemmons said.

Two years later, I asked him if he thought God had purposely decided to take Victor for a reason.

"Not my God! My God wouldn't take a 15-year-old boy in the prime of his youth," Clemmons answered.

"I don't question God. We have a good relationship, but there is no way He would have taken D," he continued.

Clemmons was going to the University of Alabama to become a doctor, and his faith-based belief in God could have conflicted with his scientific background. His conversation with me led me to believe that they intertwined without conflict.

What role did the will of God play in the death of Victor? Was it simply a one-in-a-million chance occurrence, or was God playing a direct role? Did God want to make people wake up, and used Victor's death to do so?

I was inclined to agree with Clemmon's philosophy, although we may have been in the minority when it comes to the philosophy of the will of God and the hand He had in the death of Victor. The opinions of most people who loved Victor were very strongly rooted in the faith-based philosophy of Christianity, and many of them believed it was God's will that Victor was taken from this earth.

My faith as a born-and-raised Southern Baptist has been challenged over the years, and I have become a somewhat hardened dissident of the church, as well as a cynic about religion in general. Numerous times I witnessed the church become a playground for opportunists to take advantage of the weak and desperate, as well as witnessing the multitude of good that most churches do. I admit I forget the good sometimes, as I feel the church should be perfect, forgetting that a church is full of humans who make human mistakes.

God and religion just don't seem to go hand in hand at times, at least in my eyes.

I was convinced that man is in charge of his own destiny and life, albeit a mysterious journey, and is completed with his daily choices eventually determining his ultimate fate. God simply created this environment and stays out of the way to let us make choices.

The death and life of Victor, however, would make me seriously rethink my faith and my philosophy.

DON'T CRY ANYMORE

A soft voice awakened her. She thought it was a dream at first and tried to roll over and make another feeble attempt at sleep. But the voice had been recognizable, and with each word a smile came to her face. It was three weeks since Victor died, and she was certain he had come back to visit her.

Just as she had done every night since he passed away, Cheryl had cried herself into some form of a restless sleep. Lying in bed with her eyes half shut, she heard him speak in a comforting tone.

"Momma, wake up," the heavenly voice of her lost son gently commanded.

She wasn't afraid, nervous, or emotional. Simply curious and certain that he had something important to tell her.

"Go to my room and read my Bible, Momma. I don't want you to mourn my death. Just read the book of *John* and you will understand. He finished his sentence and vanished as mysteriously as he had appeared.

Cheryl slowly sat up and looked at her clock. It was 3:00 A.M. She walked into Victor's room, which had remained unscathed since his death, and found his *New American Standard Bible* sitting on his nightstand.

He had been studying his Bible more intently weeks before his death, and she was curious to find out if something in it might help her understand. Could there be a missing clue to her son's death in this testament of *John*?

A page marker was left in the Bible. She opened it and saw verses underlined with an ink pen. She began to read the verses, which were sporadically marked through Chapters 14-17 in this book of *John*.

> ***Do not let your heart be troubled, nor let it be fearful.***
>
> ***You heard that I said to you, "I go away, and I will come to you, If you loved Me, you would have rejoiced because I go to the Father, for the Father is greater than I.***

Now I have told you before it happens, so that when it happens, you may believe.

This is My commandment, that you love one another, just as I have loved you.

Greater love has no one than this, that one lay down his life for his friends.

A little while, and you will no longer see Me; and again a little while, and you will see Me.

I glorified You on the earth, having accomplished the work which You have given Me to do.

When she finished reading the verses he had marked, Cheryl's face was covered with an angelic glow, the glow that only proud mothers have when their children do something special, something incredible.

She closed the Bible, first gripping it firmly and pulling it to her heart, and then went back to bed, sleeping soundly for the first time since his death. Her son was at peace, and she would be also, if only for one full night of sound sleep.

Cheryl knew Victor was in heaven. If heaven didn't have him, then no one would ever enter its gates. But now she had more peace than ever before. These verses, which her son had studied and underlined, seemed to tell her he was prepared to go to his Heavenly Father.

She was at peace with his presence in heaven, but I wanted to know if these verses meant something more. I continued to ask myself philosophical questions day after day:

- Why had he underlined these verses?
- Did Victor know he was going to die?
- Or were the underlined verses simply a random occurrence?

- Did Victor really come back to see Cheryl?
- Or was this just another hopeful dream for a parent who had lost a child?
- Did God take Victor for a reason?
- And if so, what was the reason?
- Does God even exist?
- Or is it simply something we dream up, especially in our times of desperation and need?

If only there were definitive answers to these questions - our lives would surely be simpler. But yet it is the mystery of God that enhances all of our journeys.

GETTING RIGHT WITH GOD

"I have to get myself right with God. It is the only way I can guarantee I see my son again," Cheryl told me the first day I interviewed her, several months after his death.

"As a mother, I hate the feeling of having no control. I was totally helpless when D was dying. All I could do was pray. It was completely in the hands of God," she whispered, as her voice began to crack.

"I am not a religious person, but yet I am very spiritual. My personal faith and belief in God is strong, and I know that God has a plan for all of us. When it is your time to join Him, you have no control. That is the hardest thing for me, as a mother, to come to grips with the fact that as my son lay dying, I was totally helpless," Cheryl continued.

"At 5:00 A.M., a few weeks after D passed, I was lying in his bed trying to sleep."

"When he first passed, I spent many nights in his bed, just to feel his presence. You know, to smell that smell of your child - that aroma only a parent can distinguish, that smell and sense that he is yours."

"I was in a restless sleep, when his radio starting blurting out, 'I Love You, I Love You, I Love You,' so loud, it woke up everyone in the house," she reminisced.

"People might think I'm crazy, or hallucinating at times, but I don't care. I cherish the times God has allowed D to send me messages. It makes my faith stronger. I know I will join him one day," she finished.

As I stood up and began to say my goodbyes, I remembered the first night I met Cheryl. It was the day Victor died, and Dr. Bryant had taken me to her house. I had walked in as an uncomfortable stranger, and she had welcomed me with a gracious hug and huge smile.

"I know you. D kept saying this week, 'The coach from Kentucky is coming, Mom.' You're him, aren't you?" she asked.

"Yes, ma'am. I am," I replied.

"I'm so sorry for your loss."

"It was God's will," she replied as she walked away to greet another visitor.

God's will? How could God take a 15-year-old young man from this earth in the manner he just had, in front of several of his teenage teammates? What kind of a God would do that?

"Look, Mom! D is scoring another touchdown," Cortez yelled, as he played the popular Playstation football game, with an imaginary D wearing the #8 and making spectacular run after run on the television screen.

"Go, D! Go!" Cheryl yelled, as if Victor were playing the game live on television, rather than an imaginary figure created by modern technology.

I walked out of the house with a strange feeling in my heart. Was the family in a state of shock, or did they know something I didn't? There was sorrow in their eyes, but also jubilation in their hearts. Throughout my life I had never experienced anything but sadness at the death of a loved one, and when people said they were in a better place, I would often acknowledge the statement as if I agreed, when in reality I didn't.

One thing was for certain as I left Cheryl's home for the first time: There was a special presence of faith, belief, and spiritual belonging that made an impression on me. I wanted to know more.

LAY DOWN HIS LIFE

Most of Victor's friends were congruent in their beliefs as to why he was tragically laid to rest at the tender age of 15.

"It makes me sad, but I have to accept it as God's will," Natalie Boone said.

"Everything happens for a reason, and although I'm not sure what the reason is, I'm sure that God had a reason for taking D," said former Hoover linebacker and teammate Matt Joiner.

"When D first passed, I was angry at God. I blamed Him!" Jonathan McCain said.

"It took me almost a year before I understood one of the reasons God took D was as a gift to me. I was going down the wrong path and heading into trouble when D was snatched from this earth.

"Each day that my struggles with depression took me near the brink of disaster, I would visit his gravesite and reflect on his lessons. The only thing that kept me from suicide was his memory. I knew how disappointed he would be with me.

"His life kept me from losing focus, and although depression and the constant need for medication made my life miserable at times, it was his memory that kept me going.

"Finally, in March of 2005, I came to grips with my vulnerability and totally committed my life to Christ. Ten days later, I was completely off the medication I had been on for more than a year. My depression ended as abruptly as it had begun. Today I am attending Southeastern Bible College, preparing for the ministry," McCain said.

"Jonathan and D were much more than friends. There was a magical chemistry between them that comes once in a lifetime. The boy you met with the eyebrow-piercing was struggling when you met him," Jonathan's mother Julie said.

"D supported Jonathan throughout his struggles, even after his death. Had D been alive, would he have been able to help Jonathan as much as he did in spirit after his death? I don't know. Yes, God and the Holy Spirit were ultimately responsible for the change in Jonathan's life, but I believe They used his sacred friendship with D to achieve this goal," she concluded.

"Coach, read his bible. Cheryl has it bookmarked," McCain finished.

The verse McCain had requested I read was the passage from the *Book of John,* which said, "Greater love has no one than this, that one lay down his life for his friends."

Had God taken Victor so his friend, or friends, could be awakened to change their lives?

McCain has certainly continued to build on this belief, with continued focus on living a good life and making a positive difference, something he was struggling with before, and immediately after, Victor died.

Jon Dunham follows his close friend McCain's belief, even though admitting there was a time when he was so angry at God, he stayed away from church for a year. As time went by, he came back to the church and also made a decision to remember Victor's positive effect on his life by having a permanent tattoo of a cross emblazed with the words "D," and "Christian," on his back.

Chad Jackson confesses he was angry at God for taking D. "It doesn't make any sense why God would take D from us at this time in life. But I must admit, every time I think of quitting, or I think I'm so tired I can't go anymore, D keeps me going. My first summer at the University of Florida, I thought about quitting several times, but each time I would think of D and work my way through it.

"I used to hope I would make it as a college player one day, and I dreamed of playing professional football. But now I know I'm going to make it. I'm playing for me, my family, and D," Jackson said.

"Each touchdown I make, I signal to D with his #8 that we are still thinking of him and to remind him he is still playing. Maybe God wants to spread his word through D by me," Jackson wondered aloud.

MISSION ACCOMPLISHED

Hunter Street Baptist Church in Hoover became the forefront for people to gather immediately following Victor's death. It is strategically located approximately a mile from the Hoover High campus, and many students had found refuge between its walls, both prior to and following the tragedy.

One of the main reasons the youth of Hoover felt comfortable there was because of the influence Youth Minister Terry Slay had on the Hoover football team. Slay had met Propst early in Propst's tenure as the newly named football coach for the Buccaneers, and the two men had instantly hit it off.

Over the next few years, Propst would visit Slay for guidance and prayer, as well as occasional advice when dealing with his players.

Friday mornings at Hunter Street would become a customary prayer breakfast and fellowship gathering for the Hoover coaching staff and football team, with Slay offering some wisdom from the word of God, as well as a brief and occasional motivational session. It only seemed natural that this would be the location where everyone who loved Victor would gather to mourn his death and celebrate his life.

I had been around Slay occasionally at Hoover games, and had even attended one of his early Friday morning sessions with the team. He had a way with young people that was persuasive yet not intimidating. They seemed to respond to his guidance and subtle lessons concerning the word of God.

Slay had never met Cheryl until D's death. His first words to her would be an attempt to answer her question, the question no minister would ever want answer: "Why did God take my son?"

"I don't know," Slay responded.

As simple as this answer appeared, it immediately perked my curiosity to hear what he had to say next. Admitting that he didn't know was not the answer I had expected to hear, and I was certain of something prophetic coming out of his mouth next.

"All I did was hold her and pray with her. Sometimes the best thing to say is nothing at all. Just love them and be there for them. Cry with them and listen to them.

"When I follow this simple reasoning of how to deal with tragedy, it is hard to mess up," Slay continued.

He now had my undivided attention, as he was one of the few men of God I had talked with who didn't pretend to know all the answers. The reality and mystery of life was kept intact with his simple yet explicit words of wisdom.

"Tony, God is Sovereign. He is over all the past, present, and future. He is also liquid and living. You can't put Him in a box, because He is always motion in purpose.

"We are born for a purpose. God wants us to live a Godly life through the Lord. D had accepted Christ as his savior and was living his life with purpose. The number of friends he had was truly unique in both variety and numbers. He genuinely cared about others, was never negative, and truly lived each day with well thought out intent, just as God wants us all to do.

"D put God first in his life. Many people inside and outside of the church give lip-service to this ideology, but D genuinely served the Lord in his daily life.

"I had never given the eulogy at a funeral until D. My mission was to let people know he had lived life the way God wanted us all to live, by celebrating each day and giving testimony through his daily actions. I was honored and lucky to be appointed to tell the hundreds of people gathered at his funeral about his purpose-driven life and how he had given us a worthy example of how we should strive to live our lives daily in serving the Lord."

Slay then mentioned the same verse in *John* that McCain, Dunham, and Cheryl had all told me to read: "Greater love has no one than this, that one lay down his life for his friends."

"Tony, we all have a purpose in life. Many of us will spend our entire existence aimlessly searching for the meaning of our existence. D not only knew his purpose, he lived it and fulfilled it. Maybe that was why he left us so early in his life. In his fifteen years he served God's mission and completely fulfilled his purpose," Slay said, as we shook hands and he walked away.

THE PEBBLE

Is it possible that God really does make daily decisions about when we die?

Does He know when we have completed our missions and purpose?

My spirituality is constantly in flux. I remember listening to radio shock jock Howard Stern, a self-proclaimed atheist, admit that if he feared death on a crashing jetliner, he would be leading the prayers to God to spare his life.

With Stern you're not ever sure when he is joking or serious, but his thought process made sense to me. We all believe in God at sometime or another. Our philosophies of exactly what God is ranges from some Muslim extremists who glorify the mutilation of Americans in the name of their god, to some Southern Baptists who believe all Jews, Catholics, and Buddhist are doomed to the everlasting gates of hell. Then there are the people on this earth like Victor, who are truly compassionate and love all people.

Interpretations of the Bible, Koran, and other religious doctrines can be as confusing as driving in downtown Manhattan during rush hour. People can screw up anything, and I have no doubt that religion, in some instances, is as screwed up as anything in this world that God created.

My belief in God has become stronger since I knew Victor. Remember, I didn't know Victor very well at all until after his death. Researching his life and studying his mission has given me peace of mind.

The God I choose to believe in has angels walking on this earth. There aren't very many of them, and when you meet them you are truly blessed. Victor was one of those angels who lived the life we should all strive for. He had a simple purpose: to be the best he could be, and to make everyone he came in contact with live a better life because of their meeting.

I don't know if God took Victor for a reason, but I do know that by his belief in God and his love of mankind and life, Victor made this world more Godly. Many people continue to carry on his life's mission because of the influence his life and death had on them.

I'm sure as he walked into the gates of heaven, the proud Heavenly Father looked at his angel and said, "Son, I'm proud of you! Job well done!"

The mysteries of God will never be answered until we leave this earth. One thing is for certain, however: If we live the life of Victor Hill, we will also accomplish our purpose on this earth. I still don't know why he was taken at such an early age, but I am comforted by the gifts his life and death bestowed on me, and hundreds of others.

When a single pebble is thrown into the middle of the pond, its ripples will eventually spread throughout the entire body of water, affecting every ounce of water and all things that live in it. Victor's life and death are a prime example of the ripple effect, and how one person can make a difference in the lives of thousands, with simple caring and good deeds for his fellow man. I think that is the life God would want us all to live.

Chapter 9

Never Over It

The phone call was similar to the many she had received the last three years.

"Cheryl, another boy died playing ball," the caller said.

She gets these calls several times a year. Sometimes the news is good and a young athlete or student is saved after going into cardiac arrest. Other times it is tragic.

The difference in living and dying is almost always the same. The ones who live had a defibrillator connected within three minutes. The ones who die didn't.

Her heart immediately goes out to the parents, siblings, and loved ones. She always offers her help. Sometimes they accept it. Other times they don't. Either way, she understands.

They all have joined her in the family that none of them ever wanted to belong. It is the most miserable family ever formed for parents: the family to which you can only belong if your child leaves this earth before you.

People try to comfort you. They will say anything. There is nothing right to say and hundreds of wrong comments. Most everyone will choose the wrong words (I know I have) unintentionally, yet still painful, instead of simply loving you and being there for your comfort.

"He's in a better place."

"We did all we could to save him."

"God needed him worse than you did."

"In time, the pain will go away."

"At least you have your other children."

"We must trust God's will."

Every statement hurts worse than the one before it. But you keep your shock and anger inside and say thank you as they move on. They didn't mean any harm; people are simply lost when it comes time to explain the unexplainable. So, they say the wrong thing.

"Simply hold us. Love us. Tell us stories about our loved ones that make us laugh and cry. You don't have to give us your philosophical belief of why it happened. You don't know and we don't know, and I certainly don't want to hear your words of wisdom if you haven't lost a child. No one can understand what a parent feels when their child is taken before them. We NEVER get over it!" Cheryl said.

Cheryl knows she makes some people uncomfortable. Some of them wish she would just go away. Why does she have to be everywhere? Sure, she has another son who is playing football, but can't she take him to another school? There are even a few people who are simply tired of hearing about her son. He's dead, and it is simply time to forget it.

Death, especially the tragic death of a teen, is a topic no one wants to face, and to see her is an unpleasant reminder that their own children are vulnerable, not the invincible creatures we would all like to think they are.

She remembers the confused stares when she brought Cortez to the school to receive his physical exam and football equipment, only days after his brother died on the field. The concerned murmurs and whispers said everything, without her ever hearing a word.

"How can she let her other son play?"

"Is she crazy?"

People get nervous when they are uncomfortable and Cheryl knows she makes people uncomfortable. Some simply don't know what to say. A few are simply tired of the occasional attention she receives from the news media and well-meaning supporters. If only they knew she would give up everything just to hold her son one more time.

MOMMA, DON'T FILE SUIT!

For the first two years after Victor's passing, some coaches and administrators were nervous. Alabama has a two-year statute of limitations on filing lawsuits, and with every day that passed there were some who held their breath, wondering if a lawsuit would be filed.

Victor died on the field, and although the effort to save him was heroic, and close to being "by the book," it was in no way perfect. Hoover was always on the cutting edge and one of the leaders in education in the Alabama school systems. It was among the first schools in Alabama to have a defibrillator, and had only recently finished a CPR training session for its coaches, but liability lawyers still would have loved to represent Cheryl in a lawsuit against the school system, coaches, and me. I knew everything wasn't perfect, and when I asked Cheryl why she hadn't followed through with a lawsuit, her answer was poignant.

"Believe me, we thought about it. Lawyers called the house and inquired about representing us. Many nights I would get frustrated and furious thinking about it. I hated you, Tony Franklin, as well as every coach and school official at one time or another. I believed you all let my son die.

"Finally, one evening a few weeks after D died, I gathered Syreeta and Cortez into the living room and we had a discussion about the possibility of filing a suit. Both children immediately told me, in a firm and passionate manner, that D loved Hoover High and those coaches, and that he would never forgive me, or see me in heaven, if I sued them.

"That was the end of that thought process, and we never considered it again. My son loved everything about Hoover, and I couldn't allow myself to desecrate his memory," she concluded.

In a world where lawsuits are filed faster than popcorn popping in a microwave, Cheryl's decision not to sue was extremely unusual. In a high profile case of sudden death in an athlete at Florida State University, the parents eventually filed suit and settled out of court for more than a million dollars. Many other cases had similar results. The last thing a public institution wants to get into is a closely watched legal fight with the family of a deceased student-athlete, especially when he is extremely well-liked and has no dirt in his background.

I strongly believe that Cheryl, no matter how efficient the school system had been, would have eventually received an offer of financial settlement from the Hoover School System if she had decided to take that avenue. However, something was more important than money to her and her family: the legacy and perceived wishes of her son.

More than eighteen months had passed when I first approached Cheryl about writing this book. She was elated at the prospect of having her son's legacy secured in the minds of people throughout the world. That was one of the reasons I chose to write the book. Her son's legacy was more important to her than the possibility of receiving money in a nasty legal battle or settlement.

It was approximately two months before the two-year statute of limitations expired on the night I asked her why she didn't file a suit. The next day I met with Propst and several of his assistants before heading back to Kentucky, and related the story of Cheryl's explanation why she had never filed suit. There was a general consensus of relief in their eyes. Although there was a belief that they had done their duties to the best of their abilities, they knew, just as I did, that it wasn't perfect. Victor died under all our care, and we all shared some responsibility.

Although there was a period of time when confusion caused some Hoover administrators to believe they were being sued, it never happened. The close personal relationship that Propst and I had experienced since 1998 suffered from the misinterpretation so much so that we ceased communicating.

I didn't interview Cheryl again until June 25, 2004. Two years and a day had passed since Victor died. The statute of limitations had now passed. She could never file suit.

"My son's wishes were fulfilled. D truly loved those coaches and Syreeta had a wonderful school experience at Hoover. Cortez deserves the right to have the same satisfying learning experience that D had without fear and unnatural scrutiny.

I'm disappointed that people don't understand, but I guess it is simply human nature.

"Since the two-year window has come and gone, it is interesting to note that there seems to be a sense of relief in some of the school officials when they see me now. Some people still don't understand why I never sued. My son loved Hoover and we respected his legacy."

My relationship with Propst continued to be strained for many months. Things were said between the two of us that caused pain, blame, and confusion. We went from talking on an almost daily basis to not talking at all. A couple of other non-related issues had also damaged our relationship and I was sure we would probably never be close friends again.

I was sitting in Cheryl's house one night several months later when she asked me about Propst's and my relationship. I told her we basically didn't have one anymore, but we would still work together to finish the book.

"Tony, D loved Rush, and I love you both. I want you both to forgive each other for what has happened. It hurts me to watch you not be friends," she implored.

"Cheryl, I have a hard time forgiving. There are things in our relationship that will never be the same. It is okay. We don't hate each other. It is just not a relationship worth working at any longer," I responded.

"Tony, don't do this for me, or yourself, or Rush. Do it for D! He loved Rush, and he would have been hurt to see you both in pain," she said.

"I'll try," I promised.

Cheryl had a way of getting to me. Victor was an incredibly gifted and special young man, as we all know now, but someone had to teach his lessons in caring, giving, loving, and humility.

Throughout the process of researching and writing this book, she had become my teacher, just as she had taught her son.

I called Propst on the way home, and we talked. It was a start. Today, we are back to our old sorry selves and have re-established a relationship: the same one as before, where we love and hate each other daily, just like brothers. If not for Cheryl, neither one of us would probably have a good friend. No one else would have us.

MORE COURAGE THAN ALL OF US

Coaches will sometimes scream at Cortez, occasionally in a tone that questions his courage and challenges him to become more aggressive. They might even question his focus, for not knowing his assignments. It's a typical day in the life of a football coach, especially in the state of Alabama and a few other football states, where coaches can still "coach hard" (another way of saying "verbally challenge") their players without the fear of being fired or sued. It is one of the reasons I love coaching here. Alabama high-school parents and fans still understand it is a violent, tough, and physical game that calls for hard-nosed coaching at times.

There is too much political correctness in school systems, but the football fields of Alabama are still one of the few places where it is thrown out the window. Most of the coaches understand the privilege they have in coaching football in a state where its importance is still valued by many as a lifetime learning experience, second to none.

Cortez is a 15-year-old freshman preparing for his upcoming sophomore season as a varsity player; the same age Victor was when he died on the field. It is near the end of May, 2005, and spring football practice is almost over. Propst called me at the end of the first week of practice to tell me how well Cortez was performing. But these last few days he had taken a step backwards after changing positions from the X receiver to the Z receiver. He seemed distracted, and with good reason.

Only two days earlier, 21-year-old point guard Danny Rumph, from Western Kentucky University, died while playing a pick-up game of basketball in his hometown of Philadelphia, with circumstances eerily similar to Victor's death. A day later, Colin Ponder, a 17-year-old Wenonah High School basketball player, in the Birmingham area, died in PE class under similar conditions. Both stories were being covered by the media.

Do you think when Cortez hears Cheryl talking to friends or the media about another sudden death of an athlete, his heart doesn't go numb or skip a beat, as the memories of his brother's tragedy flood his mind again? Cortez may be legitimately challenged by coaches for busting an assignment, but I certainly would hope challenging his courage is never an issue even remotely discussed. Simply putting on a uniform and playing the game is a show of more courage than most of us who coach for a living have ever experienced in our lives.

Many of the coaches for Hoover today are new, as several of Propst's top assistants have left to continue their careers elsewhere. Luckily, most of this 2005 coaching staff didn't watch Cortez's brother take his last breath and gasp for air while paramedics and coaches pumped and shocked his heart, attempting to bring him back to life. That horrific picture isn't permanently planted in their memories. Every time a player goes down and gasps for air, they aren't wondering the thoughts, or seeing the pictures in their mind, that those of us who were there still see. Propst admitted to me once that if he had been on the field that day and watched Victor fighting for his life, he might not have been able to coach with the same fearless intensity he still coaches with today.

I waited until nearly three years after Victor's death to interview Cortez. He was only 12 when Victor died, and I wasn't sure he would be able to handle it when I first began my research. Cheryl assured me he was a mature 15 years old and gave me her blessing to sit down with him and Syreeta in May of 2005.

MY BROTHER D

"I miss having my big brother around, especially to run to for advice. I know he could help me in dealing with being a varsity football player for the first time, as well as just talking to me about life and calming me down sometimes. He could teach me how to deal with the level of intensity the coaches have at the varsity level. I'm much more emotional than him and blow my stack sometimes.

"D was my guardian angel. He included me in everything. from being the ball boy at Simmons Middle School to taking me to the weight room and teaching me how to work out. It was okay for him to pick on me, but he made sure no one else ever did." Cortez paused for a second, and then continued.

"I cried for a few weeks, until one day I decided I wasn't going to cry anymore. D always wanted to play pro football, and I believe he died doing what he loved and is playing pro ball in heaven now.

"He had no fear in life, or on the field, and I'm not going to let fear keep me from playing. I never thought about not playing football because of his death. Nobody really knows why he died, and I have been checked out by cardiologists and other physicians and each one has given me the clearance to play.

"We recently had an isolated incident in the football locker room where someone (still being investigated at the time of this writing) painted a racist symbol on all the black players' lockers. What was amazing was they skipped D's locker. I guess that is the ultimate compliment when even a racist, or vandal, respects your legacy.

"I'm proud of what my brother accomplished, and I want to respect his legacy by continuing in his footsteps. I actually had to fight to wear his number in middle school, and I want to make him proud when I take over his locker and number this fall. The older players know how much it means, and they keep telling me '#8 is coming back,' I can't wait," he quietly said as he yawned and headed to bed a few minutes after midnight.

A SISTER'S LOVE

"I don't want him to play football. I'm scared. He's 15, the same age as D was when he died," Syreeta paused as the tears began to roll down her face.

Cheryl walked over and her put her hand on her 22-year-old daughter's shoulder and gently patted it.

"I'm sorry, Tony. I am very emotional and I still cry and go into a deep depression at times. That was my little brother and we were really close. We used to lay awake at night and talk through the vents. His bedroom was right below mine, in the basement."

"Sometimes I would say, D, you awake?

"He would answer, 'Yeah.'

"Come here. I need to talk to you.

"A few seconds later, he would be in my room asking me what I needed," Syreeta continued with a glow on her face replacing the earlier tears.

"Get me a soda.

'That's all you wanted,' he would say.

"Yeah!

'Then he would walk into the kitchen and return with a soda, and a big grin on his face knowing I had suckered him again.

"We would have our occasional brother-sister fights and he would always stay calm while I yelled and screamed. But a day later, we were always back to normal," she continued.

"The thing I'm proud of the most was his composure as a man. He never lost his cool and was always level-headed. He didn't have any enemies," she concluded.

KILLING RUMORS

2002-0755 — CASE SUMMARY

Mr. Victor Hill was a 15-year-old black male who collapsed minutes after beginning a football practice. Medical evaluation revealed no evidence of hyperthermia. The 430 gram heart showed concentric left ventricular hypertrophy. The enlargement of the heart is in keeping with the decedent's robust physical condition. Toxicological analysis revealed neither ethanol, drugs of abuse, nor illicit anabolic steroids in the decedent's system.

It is my opinion, based on the circumstances surrounding the death and the findings at autopsy that Mr. Victor Hill died as a result of a cardiac dysrhythmia of undetermined etiology. The manner of death is natural.

Gregory G. Davis, M.D.
Associate Coroner/Medical Examiner

AUTOPSY FINDINGS

1. Decedent collapsed and died suddenly during football practice.

A. Heart 430 grams with concentric left ventricular hypertrophy.

B. No definite anatomical cause for death found at autopsy.

C. No toxicological cause for death found at autopsy.

CAUSE OF DEATH: Cardiac dysrhythmia of undetermined etiology.
MANNER OF DEATH: Natural

Young people don't just die. There has to be a reason. You read the autopsy report above, and try to imagine being a parent and seeing there is no reason, or cause of death. You are elated that your child didn't do drugs, but you are stunned to find there really was no reason for his heart to stop. It just did.

We all jump to assumptions and look for reasons to explain each phase of life that deems to be unexplainable, but some things always remain a mystery. Before the autopsy report was released, people searched for reasons and some even used the death as an opportunity to push their own agendas of jealousy and spite.

Paul Finebaum's #1 rated syndicated sport's talk-radio show had the phone lines full as he received call after call from rabid football fans, Rush Propst haters, and even some legitimately concerned people with intelligent questions.

The rumors were swirling within minutes after Victor's death that the occasionally referred to "evil empire"(you earn nicknames when you consistently win championships), otherwise known as Hoover High School, and their Darth-Vader leader (Propst) had finally been exposed. Everyone knew you couldn't have the incredible and rapid success in building a football dynasty without cheating. Not only was Propst illegally recruiting players (the normal rumor when someone comes to a program and immediately wins big), but he was feeding those boys a whole lot more than beans and cornbread.

It had to be steroids. That was the consensus conspiracy theory being debated, and the fact that Hoover was one of the few high schools in America that had mandatory random drug testing for its athletes, and that no evidence existed to prove their point, didn't stop the conspiracy theorist from calling Finebaum in an attempt to spread the rumor. Within days, television, radio, internet chat rooms, and newspapers had joined in the conversation to mention the possibility that steroids might have played a role in Victor's death.

Finebaum is a legend in Alabama, having built his reputation as a fearless reporter who's never afraid of a good story, regardless of whom it may involve. Since moving into the talk radio genre several years before, his following has swelled to near "cult-like" status. *Sports Illustrated* recently named his show as one of the top twelve sports talk shows in the country, and for years he has been listed as one of the most powerful figures in the Southeastern Conference. There has never been an issue he was afraid to tackle, and this discussion had some merit simply from the standpoint that society had made steroid abuse in athletes a major concern. His show was the perfect place to debate the theory of drug use.

"Very soon after Victor collapsed, I began to receive some phone calls from people who claimed to be insiders. They were certain that Hoover players were taking steroids with the consent of Propst. I didn't know Propst that well at the time, and I believed the issue of steroids was worth discussion," Finebaum relayed to me in a phone discussion in April of 2005:

"Within a short period of time, the rumors grew into frenzy, and I let it go longer than I should have. I wasn't aware at the time of what I now suspect to be true, that some people had a specific agenda to hurt Propst. The rumors weren't as much about finding the truth about Victor's death as they were about trying to destroy a man who had generated numerous enemies, partially because of his success.

"We stopped allowing the rumors to be discussed as factual the next day and cleaned up the misconceptions created from the original frenzy. I'm ashamed for having let it go as long as I did," Finebaum concluded.

The fact that the issue became so hotly debated turned out to be a positive, rather than a negative. Victor's autopsy report ended any doubt in people's minds about steroid use and stole the credibility of the people who chose to use the tragic death of a young man as an opportunity to pursue their own selfish agendas.

Almost every person I interviewed said the angriest they got during the days following the tragedy concerned the rumors of steroids being discussed as if it were factual, along with how their coaches were being portrayed as win-at-all-cost coaches who had no feelings for their players.

Cheryl said she was furious, like everyone else when she first heard the rumors, but as time went by and she waited for the autopsy reports, she was glad the issue was discussed. If steroids were involved, she wanted to know, and although she was 100% sure Victor wouldn't have taken any drugs, she had to have proof. The autopsy report was released to the public, and the people with agendas would have to move on to another issue, as the topic of steroid abuse in Victor's death was put to rest.

GIFTS OF LIFE

Ron Swann walked into Cheryl's house with a gift. It had only been two days since Victor passed, and the funeral was soon. He held out his hand and handed her his state championship ring from the 2000 season.

"I want you to keep this. D deserved, and wanted, a championship ring much more than I did," the Hoover athletic director said.

Cheryl was genuinely touched as she held the ring close to her heart. She knew how much Victor wanted to wear that ring, and she placed it in his casket, allowing him to have it, if only momentarily. She removed it prior to the placement of his lifeless remains under the ground and had every intention of giving it back to Swann after the funeral.

Twice, she would go by to visit Swann and take the ring back to him, as she knew how much a State championship ring can mean to a coach, especially the first one. Swann always refused to take it back. He was a man of conviction and believed it was Victor's, not his.

Swan recently retired as the Hoover athletic director and works for the Alabama High School Athletic Association. His legacy will be as a man who guided the school to many championships, but his thoughtful leadership and unselfish gesture during this emotional time was the legacy Cheryl would never forget.

People can be genuinely good when their hearts are touched. Cheryl recalls countless stories of the "Hoover family," providing her with moments of love and comfort. From the carefully crafted #8 necklaces created by Beth Hartloge (B.T.'s mother), the prayer meetings and numerous visits organized by Julie McCain (Jonathan's mother), and Terry Slay, to the army of parents who formed groups to bring daily meals to the family, people's genuine goodness appeared.

Everything wasn't perfect, and there were hurtful moments as well, but overall, Cheryl's faith in human nature was replenished.

The most important group of people who helped her survive was her family and lifetime friends. So many names exist that by mentioning one she would surely leave out hundreds. After the Hoover family was finished with their kindness and short-term assistance, Cheryl's lifetime family and all her dearest friends remained on call and available on a daily basis. It continues today.

"The kindness and positive deeds are things I will never forget. So many people loved my son that my heart is eased by the fact that he meant so much to so many people."

"You live life daily and deal with the issues. Laughing, crying, and all the other human emotions remain. But there is an emptiness that never leaves you for a moment. You are never over it!" Cheryl reminded me once again as I left her house after my final interview.

Cheryl joined famed Birmingham surgeon and humanitarian Dr. Larry Lemak's First Response Team a few months after Victor's death. The team offers assistance and counseling to families who experience the tragic death of a child.

Chapter 10

29 Victor–ies!

Victor Hill didn't save a drowning child. He didn't rescue a store owner while he was being robbed, or donate $10 million dollars to charity. He didn't stop a rape in progress, or shoot down enemy forces in Iraq. He never won the MVP trophy in the Super Bowl, or hit the winning home run in the World Series.

His life was simple-yet profound, and unnoticeably heroic. It took his death to open our eyes to just how uniquely special his influence had grown in only fifteen years on this earth.

He was an African-American male raised by a loving and successful professional mother, who became a good high-school athlete. He lived each day to the fullest extent possible and made a positive effect on this world through his simplistic lessons exhibited in his daily existence. Few people could have imagined the impact he had in his brief time here. It took his death for many of us to understand that through simple acts of good he made everything he touched better. All of us who knew him, even those like me who didn't know him well until after his death, were never the same because of his gift: the gift of living and loving each day as if it could be your last.

He never played in a state-championship game and his middle-school team had trouble winning a single game, but his life was full of victories.

Writing his story has taught me things about life that I never knew, or worse, had simply chosen to forget or ignore. Victor's teammates won twenty-seven games and back-to-back state championships in the seasons of 2002 and 2003, the years he would have been a junior and a senior. It is my belief that Victor went undefeated at the same time. His twenty-nine victories came as a result of his life, and his tragic death.

The twenty-nine victories of Victor Hill are worth remembering. I hope this will help us all remember them.

VICTORY #1

Never leave the sight, or voice, of a loved one without telling them you love them.

Cheryl will always have the memory of telling her son she loved him, and hearing him tell her the same, the last two times she spoke to him. It may seem silly, but when they are gone, we all wish we had told them one more time.

VICTORY#2

The simplicity of life is what can make each moment magical, if you only take time to notice.

Who would ever have thought that the simple act of teaching someone to spit a loogie could add value to the life of another human. Natalie will never spit again without a smile that warms her heart. Magic is in the heart, and because of Victor's numerous magical moments, his wizardry continues to pay priceless dividends for others.

VICTORY #3

Each day, each event, and each person deserve the simplest act of kindness. It takes no effort and the results can make a difference that last a lifetime.

I guarantee you there is someone out there today who will read this book and smile a warm smile as they remember a day Victor walked into their lives and his warm greeting and sincere concern about their life helped them turn a bad day into a good one.

VICTORY #4

"Do good" when no one is watching.

When we do something good, we instantly want and need acknowledgement (I know I do). But as life passes by we sometimes pass up opportunities to do good because we know no one is watching. Victor flew beneath the radar, and many of his daily good deeds were never acknowledged until his death. He was one of those rare people who did good with no intention of trying to draw attention to himself. His satisfaction was in the gift of giving, and he had no expectation of receiving anything in return.

VICTORY #5

Love can truly transcend racial prejudice and boundaries.

Tammy Groce, Julie McCain, and Beth Hartloge are middle-aged white women who live in the South, where racial differences and prejudices are still available for them to witness. When Victor died, they became a part of his family to assist in any way they could. There was no color. It was simply about love. Victor played football and went to school where the majority of the students are white. His funeral, as well as his life, transcended race, as the whites at his funeral loved him just as the blacks. His love overcame racial boundaries. The only people who ever noticed he was black were the adults who never knew him. His peers simply knew he was "D" - someone who made their lives better for knowing him.

VICTORY #6

Stop and smell the flowers. You may never be at this junction again.

Have you ever stood in two places at once? What a feat! Straddling two county lines with this huge grin on his face, Victor accomplished something remarkably simple, yet when he went home that night he probably had a huge grin on his face as he marked off his mental to-do list, one more simple victory!

VICTORY #7

Don't quit when your passion tells you this is your life.

Brandon had two straight days of another human dying in his hands. For a doctor, that might become part of the job, but for an athletic trainer, it is almost unheard of. The idea of quitting should have crossed his mind. Something inside him kept telling him there was a reason for him to keep on, regardless of his pain. When Ashley went down, and his actions saved her life, he knew his passion was right. Victor's death prepared him for that moment.

VICTORY #8

Adversity can form a team that never breaks up.

Most teams could never handle losing a teammate and continue with the intensity required to be champions. Victor's teammates formed a lifetime bond of commitment that led them to championships on the field and will lead them to the same results in life. With each adversity they face, their minds will be able to replay the experience of their championships and how teamwork allowed them to overcome tragedy. Teamwork never failed them.

VICTORY #9

The mood you are in is a conscious decision. Choose to be in a good mood!

The mood we are currently in, the one we will be in one hour from now, one day from now, and one year from now is controlled by one person: ourselves! Several of Victor's closest friends told me they had never seen him in a bad, selfish, or harmful mood throughout their relationship. He made a conscious decision each moment of each day to always be in control of his emotions and moods-leaving nothing for others to manipulate or control in his life. Regardless of the circumstances, we can, and should, choose to be in a positive mood.

VICTORY #10

God is alive!

Every time my common sense begins to question the existence of God, He will remind me of his awesome power and force. I don't believe He sits in His chair and makes daily decisions about exactly what someone needs to do in life, but I have no doubt He can unleash his power at will and remind us of His will for us to do good. Much good will be done on this earth for hundreds of years to come because of the work of one of His servants, Victor. I am still utterly confused with the mystery of God and His work, but Victor helped remind me why I must continue to have faith.

VICTORY #11

Assume the worse and deal with the event accordingly.

Several times as a coach, I had players go down injured and would simply move the drill to continue practice while someone else attended to the fallen player. I was lucky. None of those players died, were paralyzed, or had life-threatening injuries, yet they could have. All of us who coach young people must take each injury seriously because one simple mistake or lack of urgency could give us, and an entire community, a lifetime of nightmares. As I do my consulting across the high-school football fields of America, I never look at a fallen player the same. They all have my immediate and undivided attention.

VICTORY #12

Rumors can hurt people deeply.
Restrain yourself until you know the facts.

The most painful part of the entire process of Victor's tragedy for most people I interviewed was the unfounded rumors of steroid abuse. When people entered the Internet chat rooms or called into the radio talk shows, their insistence on spreading the rumors caused extreme emotional pain to an already grieving community. Discussion is always good, but spreading hurtful gossip with the intention of causing pain can be destructive. Wait for the evidence. We have enough research available today to solve most mysteries, and the cause of Victor's death and whether it was related to steroid use was simple to solve with the results from the coroner's report.

VICTORY #13

Don't be afraid to live each day as if it might be your last. We have no guarantees.

Many of Victor's friends insisted he had a premonition about his death, and therefore he lived with no fear, grabbing each moment of each day and savoring it for its unique value. What guarantees do any of us have that we will have another moment after this one? From diving off a thirty-foot cliff, to straddling the county lines of two communities, Victor never failed to grasp the quality of life in every opportunity. Neither should we.

VICTORY #14

Truly appreciate other peoples' simple acts of kindness and make them feel special with your sincere gratitude.

Tammy Groce could look in his eyes and hear it in his voice. When he finished eating the peanut butter sandwich, his thank you was as sincere as his never ending smile. We all enjoy giving to others when we know they sincerely appreciate our efforts. When someone makes an effort to help or please us, be sincere with your thanks. I know I need to be updated with this lesson, especially with people I live with or work with. Don't take anything for granted. Sincerely be appreciative.

VICTORY #15

Make everyone feel as if they are your best friend. It may surprise you that they feel that way about you.

One of the most touching moments of my interviews in researching this book was the day Deontai Clemmons asked me how many people had told me that D was their best friend. To make so many people believe you are their best friend is a gift unbeknownst to many, yet worthy of attempting by us all. I don't know of anyone in my lifetime that died and had so many best friends.

VICTORY #16

Be there for them, and one day they will be there for you - even after you are gone.

When Jon and Jon had friends leave them behind as they struggled with their own lives at times, the one consistent friend who stuck with them no matter what was Victor. When he was no longer there to comfort his mother and she fell into the deepest despair, Jon and Jon returned the gift and appeared unannounced, eerily, as if they could read her mind. The law of returns can continue long after we are gone.

VICTORY #17

Fifteen years in this world can be enough, if we live each day with purpose.

Reverend Terry Slay told me we all have a purpose in being here on this planet. I believe him. For some of us, it can take eighty years to find our purpose as we walk around blindly, refusing to acknowledge the daily signs of goodness and opportunities to do good. Victor had no doubt what his purpose was, and every moment he lived to fulfill it. By doing so, he accomplished more than most of us will do if we live eighty years. Don't ignore the good around you. Opportunities are available every day to find our purpose - especially if we study Victor's simple goals of cherishing each moment and making each person's day better for having come in contact with him.

VICTORY # 18

Stop taking yourself so seriously and take a moment to sit back and laugh really hard at you!

When JayRay had an entire community of Hoover fans, players, and coaches rolling with laughter, Propst could have been furious with the impersonation of his character. Believe me, outside of myself at times, there are few people who take themselves as seriously as Propst does. However, he knew Victor was hanging in the clouds, bent over with laughter, and he joined in with the crowd to laugh at himself as hard as he had ever laughed at anyone. For all of us, especially those who have a power position, we must laugh at ourselves occasionally, or we will surely find a way to destroy ourselves.

VICTORY #19

Dreams don't have to die when you do.

When Chad Jackson pulls the #8 Florida Gator jersey over his shoulder pads and walks onto the Gator home field, known as the "Swamp," he wears Victor's dreams as well as his own. Former Hoover star Danny Rumley wears the #8 jersey for the Murray State Racers in respect for Victor. With each play, they proudly fulfill the dreams of their family, themselves, and a fallen friend who didn't get the chance to finish his own dreams. If we live a life that people are honored to have participated in, one of those proud participants—if not several—can continue our dreams for us. When someone falls before their time, it is up to us to follow Jackson and Rumley's lead and fulfill their dreams for them.

VICTORY #20

It's okay for big boys, big coaches, and grown-up macho men to cry.

Numerous young people told me during my interviews how their struggles with Victor's death were made easier by watching the tough macho coaches openly weep for the loss of someone they loved so much. Emotions are human, and honestly expressing sorrow can be a positive learning experience. As these young people go through life, the ability to openly express their emotion of sorrow will make their ability to deal with loss much easier than if they hadn't witnessed their role models show them it was normal and healthy.

VICTORY #21

Filing lawsuits aren't always the answer. When more good can come from not filing a suit, sit back, breathe deeply, and move forward.

One of the major reasons I decided to write the story of Victor's life was because of his family's decision not to file a lawsuit. Cheryl had no idea that one day some middle-aged white man, an almost complete stranger, would show up on her doorstep and ask for permission to write a story, telling the world how special her son was. Her decision to honor her son's legacy, and her children's wishes, was an honorable decision made for all the right reasons. She may live her life with a lot less money, but she has a story about her son's incredible life, which the whole world can now share in. That is priceless.

VICTORY #22

Stop mourning and live. I am where I am supposed to be.

The tragedy of losing a child is something I can't imagine and pray I never will experience. Moving on with life would be nearly impossible. Something must motivate and move you to continue. Your children are certainly enough to keep you going, but the tears still will not stop falling, and the sleep won't come. It took a return from Victor in the middle of the night for Cheryl to understand he wanted her to stop mourning for his death and move on with life. Remember his legacy: Live each moment to do good for others. It was his mission in life, and we should follow. We must bury our grief and not let it interfere with living our purpose.

VICTORY #23

Play every play, no matter what the score.

Many times over the last year and half, while writing this book, life has gotten in the way and I wondered whether it was worth finishing. Financial hardship, physical challenges, and occasional hints of depression battled me for my focus. With each lapse of focus, something would happen to remind me why his story must be told and why I must tell it. Victor quickly identified and overcame each and every obstacle in life because he never wanted to miss a play in the game of life. He showed up each day and played hard, even when his team had no chance of winning. Victor's stories were for me. They rescued me. I don't want to miss a play in life because his life taught me that each day can be a victory. We simply must show up, play the game, and notice the good in life. It is abundant if we take the time to notice.

VICTORY #24

We all know one fact to be irrefutable. Everyone dies someday. We just don't know which day.

Tomorrow I'm going to spend more time with my father, mother, brother, sister, aunt, girlfriend, wife, husband, etc. Tomorrow I'm going to apologize to my... Tomorrow I'm going to tell... I love them. Don't wait till tomorrow, for Victor's untimely death taught us all that we have no guarantees for us, them, or tomorrow.

VICTORY #25

Let your death be a celebration.

I have been to funerals where the minister struggles to find good in the deceased person's life, making it a very uncomfortable ceremony. Victor's death was a horrible tragedy that became a celebration of life that has continued today and will continue for years to come. If we live as he did, our families and friends can celebrate, as well as mourn.

VICTORY #26

Have a defibrillator, within hook-up capability of three minutes, at every practice, game, or workout, and know how to use it under extreme circumstances of life or death, with no waste of time.

Young people still die every day while playing on our fields, and they don't have to. Many of the sudden cardiac deaths in our youth can be prevented if they are properly attached to a defibrillator within three minutes. Victor's death should not be in vain. If you are a parent, don't ask, *insist*, that this rule is followed, even if you have to buy one yourself. Drive a smaller car, cut off your cablevision, eat at home for a year, or do whatever you have to do to have a defibrillator at your child's events. Don't let money be the reason another child dies.

VICTORY #27

Forgive! You are not that important that you can live your life without forgiving others.

When Propst and I went our separate ways in life, I decided it wasn't worth working on the relationship anymore. I was angry and hurt, and I did what I had done before in relationships in my life that were damaged: I let it end. When Cheryl insisted I make the effort to heal the friendship and forgive, I fought it for a while, but her persistence won out. Victor had to forgive all the time because he had so many best friends. Our friends will never meet our expectations all the time, and if we never forgive, we will die lonely. It should be our mission to heal our broken friendships. All of us should strive to die like Victor, with everyone at our funeral believing they were our best friend.

VICTORY #28

Be a good pebble. We have a choice.

If ever there was a person who truly was the "good pebble" thrown into the middle of the pond, with its ripples eventually making contact with every form of life in the pond, it was Victor. The ripples we make can turn everything we come into contact with into a better form for having known us, or our ripples can make people miserable. It is a choice, and if we follow the victories of Victor, the choice is made for the better.

VICTORY #29

Never take an angel for granted.

As we walk this world for the number of years we are lucky enough to survive, we will occasionally bump into an angel. Absorb them, learn from them, praise them, and engage them every opportunity you have. There aren't many and if we ignore their uncommon good, we will miss out on sharing their message to the world. I have only known two angels in my life, Victor Hill and my mother Patsy. It is my blessing. I hope his story can be yours.

THE LEGACY

On June 24, 2002, Victor Dionte' Hill died on the Hoover High School football practice field in the city of Hoover, Alabama, at the tender age of fifteen. His legacy is one of love, friendship, and living life with a purpose. We don't have to perform superhuman feats to live heroic lives. That is his legacy. Live each day with a purpose of providing comfort to your fellow man, being the best you can be, find joy in the simplest of things, and your life will have been fulfilled when your time comes.

A Message From Ashley Shepherd:

On February 3, 2003, only eight months after my classmate Victor Hill had gone into sudden cardiac arrest (SCA) and tragically died, I also went into SCA during basketball practice in the Hoover High School gymnasium. Because of the fast response from Brandon Shepherd, Matt Moore, and Lori Elgin, I was attached to an Automatic External Defibrillator (AED) within three minutes after my collapse. As a result of their decisive action I am alive today. At the time of my collapse I was fortunate that our gymnasium was only thirty seconds from the one AED that Hoover High School had.

Jimbo Parsons and Lord Piers Wedgwood also played an integral role in saving my life. In the summer of 2000, Wedgwood went into SCA while playing golf in Birmingham and was revived by an AED. Since that time, he has made it his mission to place AEDs in as many schools as possible by offering a "Links To Life" awareness golf tourney and event. One of the participants in the event in 2002 was Parsons, who purchased the AED and donated it to Hoover High School.

It is with this knowledge and appreciation for life that I ask everyone who has a child in sports, whether it is at the high-school level, the local recreation center, or your local church to read the next chapter and follow the instructions. Your decisive action to place an AED within three minutes usage of your youths' activities could help save someone's life one day. Don't procrastinate. Act today. My life is an example of what the actions of people who care can accomplish.

Which one of you will be somebody's Wedgwood and Parsons? Don't let Victor's tragic death be for nothing. Make a difference. I am certainly appreciative they didn't wait. Don't you!

Sincerely, and with gratitude,

Ashley Shepherd
SCA Survivor

Chapter 11

Do You Defib? Save Someone's Life Now!

Victor Hill died on the football practice field at the age of 15 due to cardiac dysrhythmia of undetermined etiology, and although the efforts to save him were as well-meaning as any humans could provide, there is a chance, if an AED (Automatic External Defibrillator) had been attached to him within three minutes, he might be here today. The chance for survival dramatically increases with the use of an AED within the proper time frame.

During the writing of this book, I became educated to the effectiveness of AEDs, as well as alarmed by the fact that most schools and youth organizations are not properly prepared for SCA (Sudden Cardiac Arrest). Every year, several young people die needlessly because some organization, school system, or church group has not taken the proper steps to have an AED within three minutes of *all* their participating athletes or students.

I have seventy clients (high-school football programs from coast to coast) that were recently sent an informal survey concerning their ability to use an AED to save a life. Over 90% of those responding would have difficulty saving a young person's life if SCA occurred. Some do not have a defibrillator, while others have one that is locked in the school in a location where it would take a minimum of five to ten minutes to retrieve and attach it. A few schools have one but don't take it with them when their team travels, therefore they depend on their opponent to be able to fulfill the required response times. Some have no coaches or trainers certified to use one.

With the above information hammering at my heart daily, I decided to search for a partner to help educate people to what they can do to save the lives of young people throughout the world. I only wanted to work with an organization that was nonprofit, efficient, and had a single-minded purpose of helping save the youth of our world from dying on our fields when it could easily be prevented.

With this goal in mind, I found *MomsTeam.com*; an online publication geared to providing life-saving information, as well as other helpful information, to youth sports' parents. Their mission, educational methods, and success were beyond my highest expectations. After talking with the President of *MomsTeam*, Brooke de Lench, and requesting her assistance, she graciously agreed to work together to accomplish our mutual goal of educating people on how they could do their part in saving the lives of our youth. Brooke agreed to share the copyrighted information from their web-site, *MomsTeam.com*, with the readers of this book.

If you never do anything again in your life to help others, please make this your one act of goodness and visit their website. You can, should, and will make a difference in saving someone's life, maybe your own families, by joining forces with *MomsTeam* and providing assistance to youth, middle school, or high-school sports' teams by educating yourself on SCA and providing the assistance needed to make sure no young person dies needlessly in your community.

Brooke C. de Lench, Founder/Publisher of *MomsTeam.com*,

founded *MomsTeam* in January 2000 in order to provide the estimated 41 million sports mothers' practical advice on the world of youth sports. Brooke is on the Board of Advisors for the Institute for Preventive Sports Medicine and is on the Board of Directors for the Matthew Colby Head Injury Foundation, and is the Founder/Director of *Teams of Angels*, a nonprofit 501(c) (3) charitable organization dedicated to reducing catastrophic injury and death in youth sports. Brooke is a 2002 International Institute of Sports Ethics Fellow.

In addition to running *MomsTeam,* she has spent thousands of hours researching and writing about organized youth sports and its effects on children and adults. Ms. de Lench spent fifteen years in the youth sports trenches as mother and coach of 21-year-old triplet sons, and has been a successful advertising executive, athlete, and community sports activist.

WHY I STARTED THE TEAMS OF ANGELS

By Brooke de Lench

On February 2, 2002, sixteen parents mourning the recent sports-related deaths of their children invited me to attend a meeting in Pennsylvania. They asked if I would publish additional articles about the charities they had set up in their children's memory, and to continue to provide parents and the youth sports community with current and reliable sports safety information so that no more children died while playing youth sports.

They also stressed the need for a 501 (c) (3) tax exempt charitable organization to serve as an umbrella for the private charities that they had set up to allow them to continue the important work they were doing at the grassroots level to educate people about the critical need for life-saving equipment and safety standards in youth sports. Out of these meetings the *Teams of Angels* was formed.

Since the *Teams of Angels* was formed in February of 2002, we have made much progress. A Board of Directors is in place with new members being added this year. Advisory Boards are being formed, as are Boards of Experts. Our first formal educational outreach campaign was launched in February 2004. The SAVE A CHILD'S LIFE: AN AED For Every Team was a success.

It would be wonderful if we knew that our schools and sports clubs were doing everything they could to protect our kids' safety while playing sports, but the sad fact is that, although there are some programs that are doing everything possible to save lives and reduce or eliminate catastrophic youth sports injuries, a lot more needs to be done. For instance, there are twenty-three States that do not even require coaching education of any type for interscholastic sports. Most States do not require CPR training or even basic first-aid classes before an individual is permitted to coach.

I am confident that many of you will stand behind us and step up to the plate to become actively involved in our important cause. With your help, *Teams of Angels* can do what is needed to educate parents, coaches, administrators and school boards about the steps they need to take to protect society's most precious commodity: our children.

Thank you in advance for taking the time to read this letter and for your support.

Sincerely,

Brooke de Lench
President

Q & A below provided by *MomsTeam.com*
read this information and act now!!!

AED stands for "Automated External Defibrillator." An AED is used to administer an electric shock to a person in cardiac arrest. AEDs are designed to allow non-medical personnel to save lives.

Q: How does an AED work?

A: Two pads connected to the AED are placed on the patient's chest. A computer inside the AED analyzes the patient's heart rhythm and determines if an electric shock to the heart (defibrillation) is required to save the victim. If so, the AED uses voice instructions to guide the user through the defibrillation process.

Q: Why are AEDs needed?

A: Because AEDs save lives. When a person experiences Sudden Cardiac Arrest (SCA), her heart's regular rhythm becomes chaotic or arrhythmic. Every minute that the heart is not beating lowers the odds of survival by 7% to 10%. After ten minutes without defibrillation from an AED, very few people survive.

Q: Can't we just call 911?

A: 911 should be called in EVERY emergency. However, in the case of Sudden Cardiac Arrest, even a delay of a few minutes can mean the difference between life and death. There are many reasons why an ambulance or other emergency response team might be unavoidably delayed in responding to an emergency (traffic, distance, inaccurate directions to the location, etc.), and each minute that passes reduces the victim's odds of survival by 10% or more.

Q: What is Sudden Cardiac Arrest (SCA)?

A: Sudden cardiac arrest is when the heart's normal heart rhythm suddenly becomes chaotic. The heart can no longer pump the blood effectively, and the victim collapses, stops breathing, becomes unresponsive, and has no detectable pulse. When used on a victim of SCA, the AED administers a life-saving electric shock to the victim's heart that restores the heart's normal rhythm.

Q: Is SCA the same as a heart attack?

A: No. Both a heart attack (myocardial infarction or MI) and a sudden cardiac arrest have to do with the heart, but they are different problems. SCA is an electrical problem; a heart attack is a "plumbing" problem. Sometimes a heart attack, which may not itself be fatal, can trigger Sudden Cardiac Arrest.

Q: Who can be an SCA victim?

A: Anyone, anytime. Children can have SCAs, teenagers can have SCAs, athletes can have SCAs, old people can have SCAs. Although the risk of SCA increases with age and in people with heart problems, a large percentage of the victims are people with no known risk factors.

Q: What does the American Heart Association say about AEDs?

A: The AHA strongly supports having AEDs in public areas such as sports arenas, office complexes, schools, doctors' offices, shopping malls, airports, and other public places. The AHA also advocates that all police and fire and rescue vehicles be equipped with an AED.

Q: What is the recommended treatment for SCA?

A: Defibrillation is the only treatment proven to restore a normal heart rhythm.

Q: How much time do I have to respond if someone is in SCA?

A: Only minutes. Defibrillate within three minutes, and the chances of survival are 70%. After ten minutes, the chances of survival are negligible.

Q: Doesn't CPR help?

A: Not by itself. By keeping oxygenated blood circulating through a victim's body, CPR potentially gives the victim a small amount of extra time until a defibrillator arrives. But SCA ultimately requires a shock to restore a normal heart rhythm. By using AEDs along with CPR, a victim's heartbeat can be restored and additional care given until the advanced emergency responders arrive. As a result, most CPR training now also includes AED training.

Q: Is an AED hard to use?

A: No. AEDs are very easy to use. An AED can be used by practically anyone who has been shown what to do. In fact, there are a number of cases where people with no AED training at all have saved lives.

Q: Can a non-medical person make a mistake when using an AED?

A: AEDs are safe to use by anyone who has been shown how to use them. The AED's voice prompts guide the rescuer through the steps involved in saving someone; for example, "apply pads to patient's bare chest" (the pads themselves have pictures of where they should be placed) and "press red shock button." In addition, safeguards have been built in to the unit precisely so that non-medical responders can't use the AED to shock someone who doesn't need a shock.

Q: Can the AED itself make a mistake?

A: It is unlikely. Studies show that AEDs interpret the victim's heart rhythm more quickly and accurately than many trained emergency professionals. Some AEDs have an internal computer system that have been extensively tested on thousands of normal and irregular heart rhythms to ensure that they make the correct decision to shock or not to shock. If a person is in sudden cardiac arrest, they will certainly die unless their heart beat is restored. If the victim is not in cardiac arrest, or has a rhythm that is untreatable with defibrillation, the AED will make that determination and not allow a user to administer a shock. In the rare event that a victim returns to a normal heartbeat after the AED has already advised a shock, our analysis system will recognize the change in the victim's heart rhythm and cancel the shock before it is administered.

Q: Can I use the AED on children?

A: A recent report by the American Heart Association found that, in an emergency, adult electrodes can be used to defibrillate a child under the age of eight if no other alternative is available. All AEDs have the ability to use pediatric pads.

Q: Can I be sued if I help someone suffering from SCA?

A: State and federal Good Samaritan laws cover users who, in good faith, attempt to save a person from death. To date, there are no known judgments against anyone who used an AED to save someone's life. However, there HAVE been cases where companies were successfully sued for failing to provide an AED.

Q: Has anyone been revived by using an AED?

A: Yes, many lives are saved every month.

Q: Can anyone buy an AED?

A: Anyone can buy an AED, but U.S. Food and Drug Administration (FDA) rules require a physician's prescription before the unit can be delivered.

Q: What features should I look for in an AED?

A: Look for an AED that is: 1) easy for non-medical people to use, 2) technically reliable, and 3) reasonably priced.

Q: How do I buy an AED?

A: By placing an order through *MomsTeam* (go to http://www.momsteam.com/AED_store/order.shtml for order forms). For more information, call *MomsTeam* at 1-800-474-5201 or send an email to AED@MomsTeam.com.

Q: Where can I get help implementing an AED program?

A: A detailed checklist to use in implementing an AED program can be read Visiting www.momsteam.com

Q: Where should AEDs be placed?

A: The general rule of thumb is to place AEDs so that they can be reached within a three-minute brisk walk from where the youth sports contests are being held. Consideration should be taken to account for any possible delays with elevators, complicated office layouts, and locked or secure doors.

Q: Why do schools need AEDs?

A: Schools are gathering points for many community activities, sporting events, and school-related functions. Hundreds if not thousands of students, faculty, parents and visitors file through the halls of America's schools and sporting arenas each year and cardiac arrest can (and does) strike several of them, annually, without warning. Having an AED available to treat these victims enables schools and their employees to respond to those emergencies and save lives.

Q: What kind of training is required?

A: Most of the training organizations around the country that teach CPR classes now offer additional training in the use of an AED. These courses typically take just a few hours and will provide basic proficiency for a user to perform a rescue.

Make a difference! Place an AED within three minutes of all your youth and get trained today!